CHICHEN ITZA
THE CITY OF THE WISE MEN OF THE WATER

ROMAN PIÑA CHAN

CHICHEN ITZA

The city of the wise men of the water

Producción Editorial Dante, S.A.

Román Piña Chan
CHICHEN ITZA:
The city of the wise men of the water

Originally titled: CHICHEN ITZA: La ciudad de los brujos del agua

First English edition: 1992

© Producción Editorial Dante, S. A. de C. V.
  Calle 59 Nº 548-7, C. P. 97000
  Mérida, Yucatán, México

© 1980, Fondo de Cultura Económica, S. A. de C. V.

I. S. B. N. 970-605-026-4

Cover design: Carlos Cámara

PRINTED IN MEXICO
IMPRESO EN MEXICO

INTRODUCTION

Ever since the translation of some of the Books of Chilam Balam by scholars such as Berendt, Brinton, Mediz Bolio, Roys and Barrera Vásquez, amongst others, our understanding of the history of the Itzá and of Chichén Itzá has been linked to both these sources and to archeological studies and in the main to those details which relate to the dating and to the determining of the most significant occurrences. The prevailing hypothesis, however, proposes that the Toltecs of Tula, from the state of Hidalgo, influenced the construction of Chichén Itzá, and that their influence explains the architectural and sculptural similarities between the two cities.

Relatively recently, therefore, Thompson (1970) stated that the Itzá were Chontal Maya or Putun, who dominated the trading routes around the Yucatán Peninsula, where a group of them settled in Cozumel from there moving on to the East coast of Yucatán, reaching Chichén Itzá about 918 A. D. A second group of Putun Itzá mixed with Toltec, nahuatl speakers, arrived at Chichén Itzá around 987 A. D. introducing in Yucatán the cult of Kukulcán or Quetzacoatl, which had prevailed in Tula, Hidalgo.

The hypothesis concerning the influence of the Toltec on Chichén Itzá relates to the departure of a certain figure and governor of Tula, Hidalgo, who went away to die in Tlillan Tlapallan, thought to be a region on the Gulf coast of Mexico, including Yucatán. Lothrop (1952) explained that when the Itzá and their followers arrived at Chichén Itzá in the katun 4 Ahau (968-987 A. D.), a legendary figure known as Kukulcán to the Maya and as Quetzalcóatl to the Nahua came with them, reputedly from Tula, Hidalgo, in the centre of Mexico. With his arrival the Toltec period began in Yucatán.

A number of researchers have accepted this rather general hypothesis. Some accept the idea of the figure from Tula who went to Yucatán, while others only admit the Toltec influence in Chichén Itzá, based principally on historical sources which show us that the priests of Quetzalcoaltl had the same name as the deity himself. These sources also show that there was a priest-governor called Ce Acatl Topiltzin-Quetzalcóatl who went to Tula, Hidalgo to rule the Toltecs. According to the *Anales de Cuauhtitlán*: "5 Calli (977 A. D.). In this year the Toltecs went to fetch Quetzalcóatl to make him monarch in Tollan. He was also a priest."

We know that after ruling for a certain time this governor-priest abandoned Tula and died. The same source informs us: "1 Acatl (999 A. D.). In this year Quetzalcóatl died. It is said that he no longer went to Tlillan Tlapallan to die there." The text continues, explaining that:

> Quetzalcóatl left at once; he stood up; he called all his pages and mourned with them, and then they went to Tlillan Tlapallan (the burner). It is said that in this year 1 Acatl, having reached the heavenly edge of the divine water, he stopped, cried, gathered up his train, arranged his feathered insignia and his green mask.... and then with everything calm and composed he made a pyre and was cremated...

It is necessary to point out that Tlallan Tlapallan was a celestial (or divine) region, formed between the light and the darkness, or between the "redness" (signifying the east) and the "blackness" (signifying the west). This in no way refers to the geographical region, or "place of the red or of the black" that would correspond to the red and black ink of the Maya codexes, which has been suggested in an attempt to prove that Quetzalcóatl did indeed depart for Yucatán. Instead, it suggests that on his death the governor received powers equal to those of the God Quetzalcóatl or of Venus: disappearing in the east (red, *Tlillan*) as the afternoon star and reappearing in the west (black, *Tlapallan*) as the morning star. Thus, after his cremation the priest-governor is transformed into the Lord of the Dawn, and so becomes a deified cultural hero.

It is clear that this legendary figure could not go to Yucatán. First of all, Tlillan Tlapallan was not a geographical region or place but a celestial bower situated between the east (heavenly bank of the divine water) and the west. Secondly, whilst he died in the year 999 A. D., the Itzá, who believed in the cult of Kukulcán or Quetzalcóatl, conquered Chichén Itzá in 4 Ahau between the years 968 and 987 A. D.

The religious cult to the god Quetzalcóatl originated in Xochicalco, Morelos, around the year 700 A. D. and began to disseminate by means of high priests who were given the same name as the deity. The cult reached the Maya lands along with militarism and other characteristics from the Gulf Coast cultures, in particular those such as yokes, "palmas", axe heads, scrolls and volutes in the El Tajín, Veracruz style. These styles mixed with those of the Pacific Coast of Guatemala, and continued on to the Usamacinta region. Along with elements of the Classic

Maya, the cult mixed in with elements from the Chontal Maya region or the Putun, from where the Itzá and Xiu brought it to Yucatán.

This explains how the Itzá, subjugated by the high priest Kukulcán, arrived in Chichén Itzá and how the Tutul Xiu (blue bird) cult would establish itself in Uxmal. It also explains how the Quiché worshipped Gucumatz and the Toltec, Quetzalcóatl. In other words, it is clear that there were high priests who, according to their native tongue, took the name of the same bird-serpent deity.

The cult to Quetzalcóatl and the various cultural influences from Xochicalco, the Gulf Coast, the Pacific Coast of Guatemala and from the Usamacinta region, all contributed to the development of Chichén Itzá, creating a style that we could call Maya Yucatec, which can be observed at many archeological sites in the Yucatán Peninsula. It was this style that exercised such influence in Tula, Hidalgo, as can be observed on the only decorated structure there.

It was not the Toltec from Tula, therefore, who transferred the architectural and sculptural details from their single building to the buildings at Chichén Itzá, but rather it was the latter buidings with their highly developed and older style, which influenced Tula. This suggests the transmission of those elements by the Itzá peoples who were to come to the Central Mexican Highlands about 1100-1150 A. D.

With respect to this Landa says: "This Cuculcán ...undertook the founding of another city.. [and] called it Mayapán... he lived several years in this city with the chiefs... and then returned by the same road to Mexico. On the way he stopped in Champotón ..." and Landa continues, "that after his return he was regarded in México as one of their gods, and called Cezalcouati. In Yucatán also he was reverenced as a god..."[1]

These citations from Landa could be related to certain other references from Torquemada, who informs us, "...and coming in small groups to Tullan... there they were bestowed with many presents because they were a welcomed and a respected people... with great projects and industries, and they tooled gold and silver and were very skilled craftsmen in whichever art, and were great stone masons... and also it is not known from where this nation comes..." He adds, "and these new people saw that they could not sustain themselves in Tulla, as this land was so populated, and they were able to move on and they went to inhabit Chollullan .... [and] they took with them an important person who was to be the chief *(caudillo)*

1 All quotations from Fray Diego de Landa are from the translation into English by William Gates, *Yucatan before an after the Conquest,* Dante, México (1990).

or ruler, who ruled them, and whom they called Quetzalcóatl [and who later the Cholutecas worshiped as a God]..."

The above equates well with the departure of a ruler-chief or high priest, (Kukulcán or Quetzalcóatl) who left Yucatán and arrived in Tula, introducing new cultural elements such as metalurgy, sculpture and architecture. of which the Itzá of Chichén Itzá were consummate masters. This also concurs with the arrival of the Chichimec Nonoalc and Chichimec Toltec in Tula, as reported in the *Historia Tolteca-Chichimeca*: "they arrived in Tollan with their Nonoualca *colonos* or labourers. There they abandoned them and the Toltec *colonos* separated from Tollan... After the Nonoualcas left, the Toltec-Chichimeca also left...in the year 1 Técaptl [1168] the Toltec arrived in Tlachiualtepec [of Cholollan]."

In other words, the "Nonoualca" were a coastal people related to the people of Yucatán, the Itzá, who by the year 1153 A. D. had already abandoned Tula and had settled in Cholula. Some fifteen years later, the Toltec-Chichimeca also went to Cholula. The name Toltec, or Craftsmen arose from the influence of the Nonoualca. In Torqumeada we read that: "[and so are these people]... they dedicated themselves to the creation of many good things... thus they were named craftsmen of the finest order; and in the same way, those who are teachers of any art or skill, are given the name of the natural ones, Toltécatl...taking that name primarily from the town of Tullan, which is where the Tultecas came to rest." He continues to say that the people form the lands of the Onoharlco "are neighbours of the sea, and are those [provinces, sic] that we now call Yucatán, Tabasco and Campeche; all those provinces were named...out of respect, Onohualco [or Nonoualco]."

Therefore, in our opinion neither historical nor archeological sources support the general hypothesis that the Toltecs from Tula influenced the style of Chichén Itzá. Rather, to the contrary, it was the Itzá who later influenced the Toltec. In the pages that follow we will try to bring to light more data about this fascinating problem.

HISTORY AND ARCHITECTURE

THE THEOCRATIC CITY

In Precolombian times Chichén Itzá was one of the largest and most sumptuous of the Maya centres. It was a holy city frequented for centuries by pilgrims from far flung places, who would invoke their gods in spacious squares and splendid temples that together formed a harmonious ceremonial centre. It was also the custom to make rich offerings to the *cenote* or well, where it was said that the gods and the souls of their ancestors resided. Typical offerings included copper or gold objects, jade, ceramics, weavings, painted gourds and *copal* or incense.

The famous traveller Stephens recounts that the ruins of Chichén Itzá were, "indeed, magnificent. The buildings were large and some were in good preservation."[2] He continues to say that the name Chichén is derived from two words of the maya language: *Chi*, which means mouth and *chen*, which means well, and so together the two words mean "mouth of the well". Chichén is therefore translated as "in the mouth of the well", the well referring to the sacred well of the Itzá. Itzá, in turn signifies "wise men of the water" (from the maya *its*, wise man, and *há* or *a* water), and hence Chichén Itzá was the city of the wise men of the water.

The Itzá were a people who arrived relatively late in Yucatán, at a time when there were already a number of sites in existence occupied by the Maya. Amongst these was Chichén which possibly, according to Roys, was at that time called Uuc-yab-nal (the seven Abnal). One can observe several constructions at the site built with stone mosaic, in keeping with the architectural styles of the Chen and the Puuc or Serranía, which originated in the north of Campeche.

In fact, the Chen style developed in the *milpa* (small, family plot) region of the State of Campeche (Hochob, Iturbide, El Tabasqueño etc), with influences from Edzná and Río Bec which flourished in the southern part of the Maya area. As a result the Puuc style derived from the Chen, and they later became contempory styles. It is known that in about the baktun 9.0.0.0.0. (435 A. D.) a southern Maya culture (Río Bec-Chen-Puuc) began to develop which later spread to Yucatán. This is characterised by slate ceramics, architecture based on the decoration of the facades of buildings, and an almost complete absence of stelas inscribed with initial series calendars, which are to be observed in the ancient seat of Chichén, before the Itzá period.

2   All quotations from John L. Stephens are taken from the original text in English: Incidents of travel in Yucatan, Dover Publications, Inc. New York, (1963). Unabridged republication of the work first published by Harper & Brothers in 1843.

The *Chilam Balam de Chumayel* tells us in abbrieviated form about the ancient seat before the renaming as Chichén:

> 6 Ahau was when the discovery of Chichén Itzá occurred. [435-455]
> 8 Ahau was when Chichén Itzá was abandoned. There were thirteen folds of katuns when they established their houses at Chakanputún. [672-692] [435-692]
> 4 Ahau was when the land was seized by them at Chakanputún. [711-731].1

Thus, without specifically referring to the Itzá this source gives information about a group that discovers Chichén, later abandons it after some 260 years (thirteen folds of katuns) and then settles in Champotón (Chakán-putún). These events are described in more detail in the Chilam Balam of Maní and of Tizimín which were correlated together by Barrera Vásquez and Rendón (1948). They say the following:

> 8 Ahau [415-435], was when the province of Siyan Can Bakhalal was discovered.
> 6 Ahau [435-455], was when Chichén Itzá as discovered.
> 13 Ahau [495-514], "se ordenaron las esteras" and occupied Chichén.
> For three twenty year periods they reined in Siyan Can and descended here.
> In the same years that they reined in Bakhalal. the lagoon, was when Chichén Itzá was discovered; 60 years [435-495].
> For ten twenty year periods they reined in Chichén Itzá and then it was abandoned [495-692].
> Thirteen folds of katuns passed [435-692].
> And they went to settle in Chakanputún.
> There the Itzá had there home; they were religious men.
> In the katún 6 Ahau [692-711] the land was reached by them, the ones from Chakanputún.

In other words, that a group of Maya people discovered Bacalar, Quintana Roo about 435 A. D. and that twenty years later the same people discovered the site which was later to be called Chichén. Forty years after that they settled there, and stayed for some two hundred years. After this the people abandoned the site so as to go to Chakanputún or Champotón, Campeche, where they settled. This all happened between 435 and 692 A. D. With no reference to the Itzá in the historical sources, we find that there is only a brief mention that "There the Itzá had their home; they were religious men". Here, the suggestion is that the Itzá were also in Champotón and that they lived there before reaching Yucatán.

3   All quotations from *Chilam Balam de Chumayel* are takn from the translation from Maya into English by Ralph L. Roys. University of Oklahoma Press, (1973). First ed. 1933.

These same sources also tell us that those who abandoned Chichén arrived at Champotón twenty years later, in the katún 6 Ahau (692-711). In the following katún (711-731) the Itzá reached Champotón, as is clearly stated in the sources "the lands were reached by them, the ones from Chakanputún". This implies that the Itzá had come from the southern part of Campeche, as we will see further on.

On this basis, and given that there is no other evidence sustaining the idea that the Itzá were present during the early years of the first occupation of Chichén, we must rely on the archeological data in order to understand the ancient settlement. We can observe a series of buildings which display the architectural styles and the slate ceramics of the Chen and of the Puuc, both of which can be related to the arrival of a people who discovered Bacalar and then this site, between the years 495 and 692 A. D. There are in Chichén, of course, other buildings with similar styles, some of which have lintels and date as late as 900 A. D. This suggests that the city was not completely abandoned (as seems to be implied in the Chilam Balam) but rather that only one of several groups left the site to go and settle in Champotón, from where later on the Itzá would return.

Therefore, the ancient peoples of Chichén (which would have had a different name) stimulated the construction of a first ceremonial centre, which can be observed near the *cenote* Xtoloc, one of several which used to provide drinking water for the population. Here are a series of buildings on platforms, in particular some with several partitioned chambers, in the Puuc or Serranía architectural style which was contemporary to the Chen. Amonst the most noteworthy of these buildings are the Akab-Dzib, The Nunnery (Las Monjas), the Church, the Chichanchob and the House of the Deer (Casa del Venado), all on the southern side of the Cenote. Notable temples include the Three Lintels (Tres Dinteles), The Lintel (El Dintel), The Hieroglyphic Jambs (Jambas Jeroglíficas) and others, all to be found on the side of the cenote referred to today as Old Chichén *(see the General Map)*.

The Akab-Dzib

This construction consists of a central building with two rooms, to which were added at the northern and southern ends two identical buildings, each of them with eight chambers or rooms, and a Maya or False Arch. Thus, the construction, on an elongated platform, is made up of three parts with 18 rooms or habitations. On the east facing facades there are finely cut steps and doors with lintels and stone jambs. All of these are plain or completely free of decoration apart from a pair of three member mouldings which form a frieze, so breaking the stark vertical elevation, and finishing off with a simple cornice.

On the wall of the main facade, looking at the front of the building, there is a crest or comb, decorated with geometric fret patterns on a stone mosaic base, corresponding to the Puuc style. Later, an annex was added to the central front section, on the eastern side or main facade, which gives the impression of a stairway on the Lithographs published by Stephens *(Figs. 1, 2, 3)*.

On the lintel of one of the inner doors of the building's southern section there is a sculptured priest sitting on a throne. In front of him, there is a receptacle or stove, with undisciphered hieroglyphs all round, which has given its name to the building: Akib-Dzib or "obscure writing". In several of the inner rooms there are hands painted in red on the Maya arches, perhaps relating to Kabul, god of the "heavenly or guiding hand". The date of the lintel is calculated as 869 A. D. (10.2.1.0.0.)

The Church

This building has a rectangular ground floor and consists of a single vaulted room, which is built over a low platform or plinth and framed by a plain dado in between two mouldings which rise to 66 cm in height. The main facade faces west and is an almost vertical and plain elevation, with the entrance and stone lintel in the central part. A border decorated with fret patterns runs all round the building, in between the two cornice mouldings. Above the border there is a decorated frieze, above which is another border of chevrons in ziz-zag, forming inverted triangles that simulate a serpent. All of this is within two simple mouldings, and finally a cornice completes the building.

On the frieze three masks made using the technique of stone mosaic, are of particular note. There is one on the central part and one on each corner, each with its hooked or trunk-like nose, representing Chac, the rain god. On either side of the masks there is a kind of niche containing two figures in three quarters relief, sitting on a dais or throne. These have been identified as the Four Bacabes who support the sky in each of the four directions. In the northern niche there is a winged figure with an oval pectoral hanging from a cord or rope, as also another figure with a conch shell on its back *(spondylus)*. In the southern niche one of the fig-

1. The Akab Dzib (obscure writing) in the time of Stephens.

2. (left) Rear view, of the Akab Dzib.

ures carries a kind of shell on the body and the other has a turtle carapace. Some researchers have suggested that the Bacabes are disguised as Crab, snail, Armadillo and Turtle, respectively *(Figs. 4 and 5)*.

On top of the wall of the facade is a comb which adds height to the building. The building is heavily decorated in stone mosaic, in the Puuc style. The decoration is a border with fret patterns, between two simple mouldings followed above by a frieze decorated with large masks of Chac, which is completed by the cornice moulding.

The Temple of the Three Lintels

Situated in Old Chichén, this building has a rectangular shaped podium, and one single chamber divided into three parallel rooms, with at least three doorways or openings in the main facade.

The structure is built on a podium or plinth, which has two plain projecting mouldings and a central border decorated with crosshatching and masks of Chac at the corners. There follows a plain vertical wall with demi-columns and simple cap-

4. The Church viewed from
the west.

5. The Church in the time of Stephens.

6. Temple of the Three Lintels, front view.

itals set onto the corners. The elevation is interrupted on the central facade by the doorways whose stone lintels are engraved with hieroglyphic inscriptions. A border of chevrons, forming inverted triangles like a broken serpent, runs all round the temple between the mouldings. There is a decorated frieze ending at the roof's ridge with a cornice moulding.

The frieze on the main facade is decorated in panels of crosshatching, blocks of four split or fluted columns and with a mask of Chac on each corner. On the other side there are only panels of crosshatching and fluted columns. The whole building, however, with the characteristic stone mosaic fits the Puuc or Serranía style. One of the lintels is inscribed with the date of 10.2.10.0.0. which corresponds to around the year 850 A. D., following the count of katunes rather than the initial series count *(Figs 6, 7, 8)*.

The Chichanchob

This building consists of a rectangular shaped podium or platform 22.40 metres long and 17.90 metres wide. The sloping part of the structure ends with a project-

7. (above) Detail of the frieze decoration from the Temple of the Three Lintels.
8. Rear view of the same building.

9. View of the Chichanchob (the Red House).

ing dado or moulding. It has rounded corners and rises to a height of 7 metres. In the central part of the western side is a simple staircase, 9.65 metres wide providing access to a temple above.

The temple is set on a podium or plinth framed by two cornice mouldings and a central border decorated with stone crosshatching, broken by three little steps with balustrades that provide access to the vestibule or first room. This temple has two chambers, one which serves as a vestibule (ante room) and the other as a sanctuary with its three rooms each roofed with a Maya vault.

The facade of the temple is plain and has well cut stones. It has a frieze carved in between two cornice mouldings, which lifts the height to 3.70 metres. There are two crests or combs. One of these is original and old, and is located on the central part of the roof. It features openings in the base and is decorated with fret patterns in between the cornices. The other crest, added on later, is located on the front of the facade, and has masks of Chac over the axis of the doors, decorated with stepped fret patterns *(Figs. 9, 10)*.

This building is also known as "The Red House" because of a painted red fresco that is to be found in the vestibule or first chamber. As such, Chichanchob is

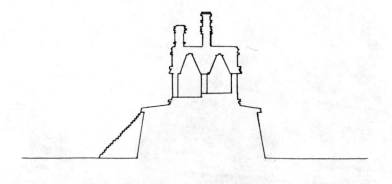

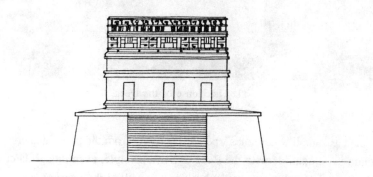

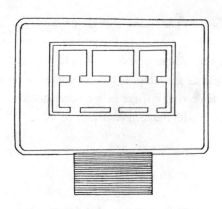

10. Plan of the Chichanchob.

11. The House of the Deer.

translated as "small water holes", perhaps deriving from the perforated crests. This structure is compatible with the Puuc or Serranía style, even though later on the Itzá built a small Ball Court on the back or east wall of the platform.

The House of the Deer

This building stands a small distance from the Red House, with architectural lines very similar to the previous building. It too consists of a three roomed temple with a plain facade, an undecorated frieze between the mouldings, and a crest built onto a platform or podium with rounded corners *(Fig. 11)*.

The Nunnery

For Stephens, who would have seen this complex in 1841, The Nunnery was most notable for its well preserved state and for the richness and beauty of its adornments. The front faces to the north and consists of three buildings: The Nun-

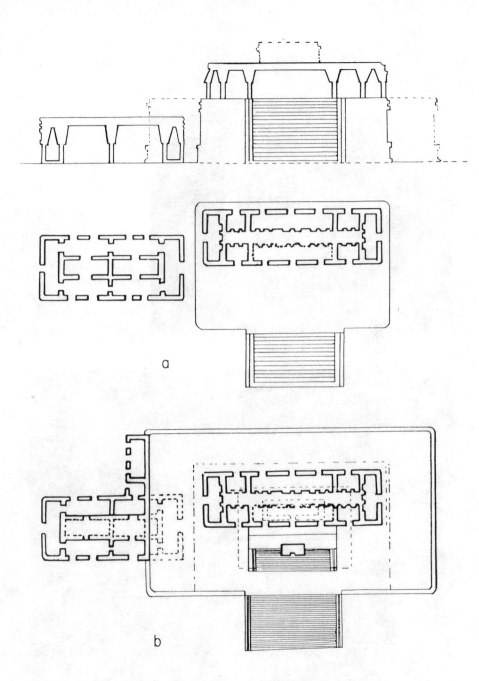

12. Plan of the Nunnery Group. a) Original base plan of the Nunnery and the East Annex. b) Base plan of the second building of the Nunnery, which covers part of the East Annex.

13. (left) Parcial view
of the Nunnery.
14. The Nunnery
Group in the time of
Stephens.

15. Detail of the facade of the Temple of the Nunnery with the stairway to ascend to the second temple.

16. Rear view of the first Temple of the Nunnery.

nery itself, the Eastern Annex and the Southeastern Annex, all of which relate to different building styles or periods, and feature superimposed structures.

The Nunnery. Originally, this building consisted of a rectangular shaped podium set on a terrace or platform that today is covered by the Church. The podium, at a lower level and now no longer visible is 33 metres long and 12 metres wide. The building has a tall structure rising to 10 metres in height, which stands on a plinth framed by simple mouldings, a vertical frieze and another wide moulding to finish off, all plain and with rounded corners. On the north side there is a central staircase with balustrades which gives access to the upper temple.

The temple consists of two large, parallel chambers with six alligned rooms or partitions with doorways facing to the north and to the south, and two independent rooms, one at each end of the building, with doors facing to the east and west, each roofed with Maya vaulting. The northern facade is decorated with panels of crosshatching, fluted columns and small squares, whilst the south face has fret patterns, fluted columns, knots and small squares, sculptured with rosettes. The style of the building with its heavily decorated facades is similar to that of the Chen. The frieze between the cornice mouldings is plain and slightly inclined giving the impression of a Maya hut. It is also possible that in earlier times there was a central crest or comb. *(Figs. 12, 13, 14, 15, 16).*

This original base or temple was next to the so called East Annex, which was an independent structure. Later, however, the base was extended, reaching 50 metres in length and 23 metres in width, thus covering part of the western wing of the East Annex and so giving the impression that this building was built into the base.

The new base has the same depth as the original, and contains a single structure with a moulded plinth, a vertical frieze and a border or wide moulding decorated with masks of Chac and panels of crosshatching, also with rounded corners. Originally, it shared the same central stair with the earlier structure, but there was some additional building, in particular a new and narrower stairway built to be able to reach a second temple that was built on top of the former.

In other words, on the original foundation two wings or sructures were added that concealed the former building and part of the East Annex. Another small temple was also built, demolishing the original crest. This new temple had a facade decorated with a frieze of fluted columns in the Puuc style. It was for this temple that the second staircase was erected, on the platform of the first building, leaving a half-arch passageway which allowed entry into the central room of the first temple *(Fig. 17)*.

The East Annex. Originally this structure had a rectangular platform about 10 metres wide and 21 metres long. It had three parallel chambers each with two rooms and doorways facing north and south. There was also a room in the east and another in the west with their respective entrances. The Annex formed a harmonious complex similar to the temple of The Nunnery, with whose original foundation this structure overlapped on the east side.

The style of this Annex corresponds to the Chen, contemporary to the Puuc, characterised by the very full decoration on the facades. Thus, on the north and south sides of the building there is a section of the facade with panels of crosshatching and two masks of Chac superimposed on the corners. Next, there is a frieze between two flying cornices, also decorated with masks of Chac on the corners and above the doorways, interlocking with panels of crosshatching. On the

17. Extension made to the first basement of the Nunnery.

upper moulding there is a serpent-shaped border of inverted triangles or chevrons, in ziz-zag.

The most majestic and elegant facade is, of course, that of the the eastern chamber. It has a plinth framed by two raised mouldings and a central border decorated with split or fluted columns and fret patterns. Next, is a section of facade where the central doorway is framed with curved or trunk-like noses of the the rain god Chac, and on each side masks of the same god, two of them superimposed on the corners. Continuing round, there is a flying cornice moulding which bends in a right angle to encompass the door, with a border of interlocking S shaped motifs signifying serpents or a plaited rope. Next follows the frieze with a medallion at the height of the door, showing a seated figure richly adorned in a headress of beautiful feathers and decorated with fret patterns. On each side of him there are two more masks of Chac. The building is completed by a cornice with a central molding or ridge.

It is possible that this building had a crest on the front of the facade, as is shown in Stephen's lithograph. On the door lintel there is a hieroglyphic inscription which has been calculated to date from around 880 A. D., according to the katun wheel, and as we have already mentioned, part of the west wing was obscured by the amplification of the second foundation of The Nunnery, which curtailed its rooms and gave the impression that this building had formed part of the other's foundation. *(Figs. 18, 19)*.

It is also probable that during the Itzá occupation this building would have been altered, as happened in Uxmal with the introduction of the cult of Kukulcán, but still conserving well the mixture of elements relating to the afore mentioned religion. Thus, perhaps a mask of Chac which used to frame the eastern doorway (in the Chen style) would have been substituted by the medallion of the seated figure that we see today, and at the same time they might have interlocked some stones representing a tail of the rattlesnake on the ends of the north and south faces, and so finishing off the moulding at the ridge of the roof.

The South Annex. This building dates from the time of the Itzá who brought with them the cult of Kukulcán and also other architectural details, such as the use of columns to support wooden lintels and jambs in bas-relief. It can be seen that the Itzá added on two rooms to the walls of the base of The Nunnery and to the East Annex, so as to enclose a small patio surrounded by other contemporary structures *(Fig. 12)*.

18. Front view of the East Annex.

19. The east facade of the East Annex in the time of Stephens.

THE MILITARY CITY OR THE CITY OF THE ITZA

The buildings briefly described above, show that the ancient inhabitants of Chichén were related to the Mayas, the creators of the Chen and the Puuc architectural styles. According to the dates on the hieroglyphic inscriptions found there, these peoples lived free from foreign influence until 900 A. D. It was not until after this date that Chichén was conquered by the Itzá, who came from the west after abandoning Champotón, Campeche.

Whilst Chichén, with its cults to Chac the rain god, was developing into a theocratic city of some importance, some of its people inexplicably left the city to go in search for other lands. It is at this juncture that the Chilam Balam of Maní, Tizimín and Chumayel begin to refer to the Itzá in their writings, who also occupied Champotón before making their way to Yucatán.

The Itzá (wise men of the water) arrived late in Yucatán, conquered and settled in Chichén, and introduced the religious cult to Quetzalcóatl, but here using the name of Kukulcán. The *Chilam Balam de Chumayel* relates the following:

> A tender boy was I at Chichén, when the evil man, the master of the army came to seize the land.
> Woe! At Chichén heresy was favoured!...
> Ho! 1 Imix was the day when the ruler was seized at Chikin-chen.
> 1 Imix was the day he said this...
> Buried, buried! This was their cry on that first day of Yaxkin, that mighty day...
> Is there perhaps anyone who by chance awakened?
> Force was brought to bear for the second time.
> Woe! For the third time was established the religious festival of our enemies, our enemies...
> Soon it will come to Chichén Itzá, <where> heresy was favoured....
> Who am I said to be among men?...
> You do not understand me. I was created in the night.
> What were we born?
> We were <like> tame animals <to> Mizcit Ahau.

This song, sung by the Halach Uinic or king [*señor, rey,* in Spanish], in the temple situated on the west bank of the sacred cenote or well, on the first day of the year (1 Imix), clearly expresses that Chichén was conquered in war and that the conquering people were the Itzá. It is also clear that they gave the name of Chichén (Rim of the well) to the place, and that they were created by the Mizcit Ahau (the god or king [señor] Mizcit). The addition of the title (Ahau) after the proper noun shows this to be a Maya-Chontal name.

In other words, the Itzá were no more than the conquering tribe who arrived in Chichén towards the end of the Mesoamerican Classic Period, after 900 A. D. They were said to have been created by Mizcit Ahau who is none other than Nacxit, Kukulcán or Quetzalcóatl, the divine-creator of the Fifth Sun and of the new humanity born in Tamoanchan. In the same way that the religion or cult to Quetzalcóatl originated in Xochicalco, Morelos, from there spreading across the Maya region acompanied by militarism and spurred on by high priests and rulers who used to adopt the same name as the deity (translated into their native languages), the Itzá in the Maya-Chontal territories, made themselves descendents of Quetzalcóatl/ Kukulcán and took the cult to Chichén Itzá.

In fact, it was through Quetzalcóatl that several tribes or migratory groups developed their lineages, and with the adoption of his cult were afforded the status of townships. In this way, the Toltec from Tula, Hidalgo, received their God by the mediation of the high priest called Ce Acatl Topilitzin Quetzalcóatl. The Etzlapictin Teotenaca adopted the god Nauhyotecuhtli (Lord or King of the Fourth or Fifth Sun or Fourth Movement, Nahui-Ollin). The Quiché called him Gucumatz or Tohil and the Itzá and Xiu called him Mizcit, Kukulcán or Nacxit, as they also called their priests. Thus, Quetzalcóatl or Venus (the man-bird-serpent) was a dual deity and was also known as Nacxitl (the Four Feet), or by other names such as Mizcit, Kukulchan, Nacxit, Kuchit, Votán, Kukulcán, Tohil, etc. according to the language of the adopting group.

It becomes clear that the Itzá believed themselves to be created by Quetzalcóatl or Mizcit Ahau. They could not have been in Yucatán before 900 A. D. because the cult of their God, Kukulcán or Quetzalcóatl (the man-bird-serpent), originated in Xochicalco, Morelos. It is also clear that the Itzá were in the area of the Laguna de Términos and Champotón —a region then known as Zuyúa— before going to Yucatán.

So, the Itzá were a people of Maya-Chontal language in the Zuyúa (western) region of Xicalango and Champotón, Campeche. They had a hybrid culture containing elements of Maya, Chontal, the Mexican Central Highlands, Central Veracruz, Huasteca and even elements from the Guatemalan Pacific Coast. They celebrated the cult to Quetzalcóatl and the phallic cult, practiced militarism, favoured the style of sloping and of vertical walls, wore clay nose adornments, yokes and "palmas" and practised decapitation. They brought this hybrid culture with them to Yucatán when they left Champotón in the company of the Xiu, who had practically the same customs.

The region of Zuyúa (Xicalango, Isla de Términos, Champotón) was apparently the home or concentration point of several groups (Quichés, Cakchiqueles, Itzaes, Xiues), who later dispersed in different directions to found their cities, beginning their lineages under the guidance of Quetzalcóatl (Gucumatz, Tohil, Kukulcán). In the *Popul Vuh* it is written:

> The names of each of them were different when they multiplied there in the East, and many were the names of people: Tepeu, Olomán, Cohah, Quenech, Ahau is how these men were named there in the east, where they multiplied.
> And the news of a city having come to be heard, they went in search of it.
> And now, the name of the place where they went... was Tulán-Zuiva, Vucub-Pec, Vucub-Ziván. This was the name of the city where they went to receive their gods.

The *Memorial de Sololá* says:

> From four [places] the people arrived at Tulán. In the East is one Tulán; another is in Xibalbay; another one is in the West, from whence we came; the other is God.

To clarify the above citations it must be taken into account that Olomán is synonymous with Olman, meaning land of rubber; Tulán is synonymous with Tollan or Tula, meaning city or place densely populated; Vucub-Pec and means Seven Peaks, and Vucub-Ziván Seven Gorges; Zuyúa means the west and Xibalbay is the yellow or southern region of the dead.

Therefore, the sources quoted above tell us that several groups travelled over the Gulf Coast lands (in the east) from the south of Veracruz (Olman) to Laguna de Términos (Zuyúa), passing by Tabasco (Nonoualco) and then on to a city (Tulán) called the City of the West (Tulán-Zuivá) in the region of the Seven Peaks, Seven Gorges (Vucub-Pec, Vucub-Ziván). They came to receive their gods in a region which we will risk identifying as Xochicalco, Morelos. The sources also tell us that other important cities were in existance, in the east, in the west, in the south (Xibalbay) and in the north (where God is).

In support of the contention that Zuyúa refers to the west and that it was situated between Xicalango and Champotón, principally in the region of Laguna de Términos, we can turn to the records of the Cakchiqueles where in the *Memorial de Sololá* we read the following:

> There is war over in the East, in the land called Zuyvá; there you will go to prove [the strength of] your bows and arrows and your shields that I will give you.
>
> Then we met up and straight away confronted the enemy tribe, the so named Nanoualcas, the Xulpiti, who were to be found at the edge of the sea and they were aboard their boats.
>
> .... soon they were destroyed by us... we embarked in the canoes of the Nonoualcas and set off towards the East and where we soon arrived. In truth, they were really formidable, the city and homes of the Zuyvá, over there in the East.... we attacked once, we attacked twice, until we were defeated.
>
> We at once spread out in the mountains; we all went, each tribe took his own path, each family went its own way.

And in *Popul Vuh* we read:

> There in Tulán, in Zuyvá, we separated, from there we set off together and there our race was created when we came, they said amongst themselves.

That is to say, that the Cakchiqueles, Quichés and other peoples abandoned the City of the West (Tulán Zuyvá o Xochicalco, Morelos) after receiving their gods. They then set off towards the Gulf Coast where they fought with the Nonoualcas from Tabasco and the Xulpiti. It is thought that these people may have been the Xiu, as they also had their home in Nonoualco. From there they moved on to Zuyvá (Zuyúa or Laguna de Términos) where they were defeated and returned, going back towards Guatemala crossing the Tacaná (Tanahuyú) mountains.

Regarding the Xulpiti or Xiu who settled in Yucatán at almost the same time as the Itzá, the *Chilam Balam de Maní* informs us that:

> This is the order of the katuns from when they came out of their land, their homeland of Nonoual.
>
> For four katuns were the Tutul Xiu [849-928] to the west of Zuyúa.
>
> The land from whence they came [is] Tulapan Chiconautlan. For four katuns they walked so as to arrive here, in the company of the lord [Holón] Chan Tepeu and his companions.
>
> In the katun 2 Ahau [987-1007] Ah Sutok Tutul Xiu was established in Uxmal.

Here we find that the Tutul Xiu (blue birds) left Tulapan Chiconaoutlan (Ciudad Chiconautlan on the coast of Veracruz or El Tajín) and made their home in the Nonoualco region (Tabasco) west of Zuyúa (Laguna de Términos). Later, some of them set off towards Yucatán, retaking and settling in Uxmal around 987-1007 A. D. It was more or less at the same time that the Itzá set off for Chichén, entering from the west, from Champotón, Campeche.

As we mentioned earlier, the Itzá conquered the land of Chakanputún or Champotón, Campeche in a 4 Ahau (711-731), according to the *Chilam Balam de Chumayel*:

8 Ahau [928-948] was when Chakanputun was abandoned by the Itzá men. Then they came to seek their homes again. For thirteen folds of katuns had they dwelt in their houses at Chakanputun. This was always the katun when the Itzá went beneath the trees, beneath the bushes, beneath the vines, to their misfortune.

We know, therefore, that the Itzá conquered and occupied the lands of Chakanputún or Champotón in a 4 Ahau (711-731) and remained there some thirteen folds of katuns, or more than two hundred years, until 8 Ahau (928-948). They abandonded Chakanputún and went to Yucatán to seek new lands on which to settle, but not before having suffered a series of difficulties.

This supports the claims that the Itzá were in Chichén and from there went to Champotón, returning to Chichén after about two hundred years. However, in that case they would not have faced any problems returning, now knowing the route and the location of Chichén very well. What we really find here is a migration of the Itzá from Champotón to Yucatán across unknown territories, occupied by other peoples, with the resulting problems for the migratory group. Regarding the migration by the Itzá, *Chilam Balam de Chumayel* says:

4 Ahau was the name of the katun when occurred the birth of Pauahs, when the rulers descended. [Thirteen katuns they reigned]

    4 Ahau was the name of the katun when they descended; the great descent and the little descent they were called.

    4 Ahau was the katun when they sought and discovered Chichén Itzá. There it was that miraculous things were performed for them by their lords. Four Divisions they were, when the four divisions of the nation, as they were called, went forth.

    4 Ahau was the katun when the four divisions were called <together>. The four divisions of the nation, they were called when they descended. They became

lords when they descended upon Chichén Itzá. The Itzá were they then called.

Thus, in the katún 4 Ahau (968-987) the Pauahs were born as they set forth from Champotón towards Yucatán, together with the god Kukulcán (Mizcit) who had created them and had made them see the light. Their lords, the Pauah or gods of the four corners of the world, penetrated from the west (the great descent), although it was also in a 4 Ahau (1224-1244) that they later penetrated in the east (the little descent). In the source it says "4 Ahau is the name of the katun" and not that it was the same as in the "great descent, the little descent as they were called". They sought Chichén in the company of four groups of people, or four divisions, named Cantzulculcab (which in Chontal means, chiefs of four partitions) and they called themselves Itzá when they conquered Chichén. The history from *Chumayel* continues:

> From Kincolahpetén in the east one division went forth. From Nacocob in the north one division came forth. One division came forth from Holtun Zuyúa in the west. One division came forth from Four Peaked Mountain, Nine Mountains is the name of the land.

According to this version, four groups with their chiefs left the region known as Nine Mountains (Bolonppel-uitz or Salinas de los Nueve Cerros on the river Chixoy, according to Roys) near the Usumacinta and Guatemala-Chiapas. Some departed from Kincolahpetén or the Low Lands, others from Nacocob, others from Holtún-Zuyúa or Laguna de Términos-Champotón and others from Four Peaked Mountain. All of them set forth towards Yucatán thus forming the Great Descent from the west.

This may also explain the spread of the Quetzalcóatl or Kukulcán cult in the Maya region, as can be observed in Seibal, Altar de Sacrificios, Aguateca (Nine Mountains, Kincolah-petén), and in Zuyúa amongst the Maya-Chontal, Itzá and Xiu (Holtún-Zuyúa). The cult is also evident in a series of cultural elements in Chichén Itzá and Uxmal. The different elements to be seen originate from different areas. From Veracruz and the central Huastec region clay nose adornments, the phallic cult, yokes, "palmas" and decapitation of ball game players are characteristic. Elements originating from Xochicalco include the cult to Quetzalcóatl, architecture with sloping and vertical walls and lords of time with the glyph of the year. Sceptre handles engraved with serpents, belts and sandals featuring knots finished with serpents and leafy motifs are typical of the Pacific Coast of Guatemala and the Usumacinta region.

In that same 4 Ahau the *Crónica Matichu* (which consists of the Chilam Balam of Maní, Tizimín and Chumayel), arranged by Barrera Vásquez and Rendón, says: "4 Ahau [968-967] For twice twenty years [they wandered] and came to make their homes, once again, after having lost Chakanputún". This reference is confirmed by Landa, who says:

> The indians relate that there came into Yucatán from the south many tribes with their chiefs, and it seems they came from Chiapas, although this the Indians do not know;.... They say that these tribes wandered forty years through the wilderness of Yucatán, having in that time no water except from the rains; that at the end of that time they reached the Sierra that lies about opposite the city of Mayapán, ten leagues distant. Here they began to settle and erect many fine edifices in many place;...

In the part of the *Chilam Balam de Chumayel* which describes "The Ritual of the Four World-Quarters", the details given for the great descent (from the west) and the little descent (from the east) seem to be confused, as they practically name all of the peoples of Yucatán in relation to the conquest and foundations of the Itzá. Archeologically, there is no evidence from the dates or the buidings, to identify them with the Itzá. We will now examine what seems to be a refernce to one or other of the "descents" starting from the migration and creation of the Itzá by Mizcit Ahau.

According to the *Chilam Balam de Chumayel* (Roys 1933):

> The logwood tree is the hut of Yaxum [green bird, quetzal), the first of the men of the Cauich family.
> The lord of the men of the south is the first of the men of the Noh. Ix-Kantacay is the name of the first of the men of the Puch family. They guard nine rivers; they guard nine mountain.
> 11 Ahau was the katun when they carried <burdens> on their backs.

And also according to the *Chumayel* (Mediz Bolio 1973):

> In 11 Ahau is the appearance of his followers.
> And Ah Ppisté came. This Ah Ppiste was he who measured the land.
> And then came Chacté Abán, to prepare the markings of the land to be cultivated.

And Uac Habnal came to mark the measurements with grasses, and then came Ah Ppsisul, the one who measured, who measured long leagues.

This was when the chiefs of the four quarters were decided.

Once Chichén Itzá was conquered and occupied, the Itzá proceeded to arrange it. With the intervention of certain Gods (amongst them Mizcit Ahau) they measured the lands for agriculture and decided the boundaries of the lands for the people who came with them. In this way the population of the Itzá gradually increased during 987 to 1047. The *Chumayel* continues:

When the sons of the bees swarmed [multiplied] the little Cozumel was the flower of the honey, the jar of the honey, the first hive and heart of the land.

Kin Pauah was the high priest, who ruled the warriors and was the keeper of Ah Hulneb, on the altar of Cuzamil.

The priests of Uxmal reveered Chac, the priests of the former time. And Hapai Can was brought in his boat. When this one arrived, they marked the walls of Uxmal with blood.

It seems that Cozumel may have been occupied by one group of the Itzá during their period of expansion, when Kin Pauah (Tun) god of the south wind, was priest. In Uxmal, where the Itzá venerated Chac, god of the rain, the cult of Kukulcán was introduced by Ah Mekat Tutul Xiu, who occupied Uxmal from 987 to 1007. Kukulcán's symbol was the beautiful plumed serpent (Hapai Can or the sucking snake) and his followers practiced militarism or warfare, which is why they marked the walls or buildings with blood.

According to Chilam Balam de Chumayel:

Ah May it was who fixed the corners of the land, he who set the corners in their places; the sweeper who swept the land was Mizcit Ahau.

[...] Then began the introduction of the tribute to them at Chichén.

[At TiKuch] arrived the tribute of the four men.

11 Ahau was the name of the katun when the tribute was handled. [1027-1047].

Then came the tribute of Holtun Zuyúa, there at Cetelac, where they agreed in their opinions.

13 Ahau was the name of the katun when the head chiefs received the tribute.

Then they began their reign; then they began their rule.

Then they began to be served; then those who were to be thrown (into the cenote) arived; then they began to throw them into the well that their prophecy might be heard by their rulers.

Their prophecy did not come.

From the above it is clear that the Itzá saw the light thanks to the Lord Mizcit. They had lands and began to receive tributes from the four chiefs who had come with them. They also received tribute from Holyún Zuyúa from where they had come and where they continued to maintain relations. In Chichén Itzá they began the sacrifice of men, throwing them into the sacred cenote or well. This practice is part of the cult or relgion to Kukulcán which they introduced, called Mizcit Ahau in the *Chumayel*.

With respect to this Landa says:

The opinion of the Indians is that with the Itzá who settled Chichén Itzá there ruled a great lord named Cuculcán, as an evidence of which the principal building is called Cuculcan. They say that he came from the west, but are not agreed as to whether he came before or after the Itzá, or with them. They say that he was well disposed, that he had no wife or children, and that after his return he was regarde in Mexico as one of their gods and called Cezalcoahuati [Quetzalcóatl]. In Yucatán also he was revered as a god, because of his great services to the state...

Landa's statement is interesting because in general the name of Kukulcán does not appear in the Chilam Balam (except as Mizcit, Ah Nacxit Kukulcán and Ah Mex Cuc in the *Chumayel*). The Itzá introduced the cult in Yucatán in the katún 8 Ahau (928-948, bringing it with them from Champotón. At this time, the Toltec of Tula, Hidalgo still had not fetched Ce Acatl Topilitzin (Quetzalcóatl or high priest of that deity) to govern them. The return of Kukulcán to Mexico where he was called Cezalcuati, implies that certain cultural elements (paintings from Cacaxztla, from Valle de Bravo, from the temple to Tlahuizcalpantecuhtli in Tula etc.) that had developed in Chichén passed on to the Central Altiplano. The so called Toltec influences in Chichén Itzá never in fact existed: on the contrary, there were influences from Chichén in Tula, Hidalgo.

Clearly, the hypothesis so long sustained by a number of researchers suggesting that Ce Acatl Topilitzin Quetzalcóatl abandoned Tula and went to Yucatán (bringing with him such architectural trademarks as columns in the form of serpents, chacmools, square columns decorated with warriors, colonnades etc.) is untenable both chronologically speaking and according to the specific styles concerned. Instead, those elements actually originated in Chichén starting with the styles developed by the Itzá, themselves based on elements from Xochicalco, the Veracruz and Huastec Coasts, the Pacific Coast of Guatemala and Usumacinta, and then passed on to Tula around the close of the Mesoamerican Classic Period.

Also, we know from Landa:

> That this Cuculcán, having entered into agreement with the native lords of the country, undertook the founding of another city wherein he and they might live, and to which all matters and business should be brought. To this end he chose a fine site eight leagues further inland from where Mérida now lies, and some fifteen or sixteen from the sea. They surrounded the place with a very broad wall of dry stone some eighth of a league in extent, leaving only two narrow doorways; the wall itself was low. In the middle of the enclosure they built their temples, calling the largest Cuculcán, the same as Chichén Itzá. They built another circular temple different from all the others in the country, with four entrances... Within the enclosure they built houses for the lords alone... Cuculcán did not call the city after himself, as was done by the Ah-Itzá at Chichén Itzá (which means the well of the Ah-Itzá), but called it Mayapán, meaning the "Standard of the Mayas".

According to the *Chilam Balam de Chumayel:* "13 Ahau [1007-1027] is the katun when they founded the city of Mayapán. Maya men they called it." And once more following Landa: "The inhabitants of Mayapán held most friendly relations with them... In this manner, the people of Tutul Xiu subjected themselves to the laws of Mayapán, they intermarried...". Thus, the Itzá formed an alliance linking Mayapán and Uxmal with Chichén Itza, which enabled the respective ceremonial centres or cities to grow larger in both size and beauty, until the collapse of the alliance or League of Mayapán by the treachery of Hunac Ceel, between 1185 and 1204 A. D. The Xiu and the Itzá arrived at almost the same time in Yucatán, around 987-1007 A. D.

The Xiu settled in Uxmal and the Itzá in Chichén, giving it their name: Chichén Itzá. Both groups introduced the cult of Kukulcán or Quetzalcóatl to the region, by means of high priest-rulers who had the same name as the deity (Kukulcan, bird-serpent; Tutul-Xiu, blue bird or Cotinga). The religious cult to Kukulcán or Quetzalcóatl came accompanied by militarism, by wars and by conquests, and flaunting a hybrid culture based on elements from different parts of Mesoamérica. In Chichén Itzá the new inhabitants erected buildings that revealed the introduction of a new religion or cult to Kukulcán (as also happened in Uxmal), in a style we will call Maya-Yucatec. Amongst these buildings are the Ball Court, The Caracol,

the Temple of the Bearded Man, the Substructure of the Castle, the Temple of the
Tigres and several others.

The Ball Court

This structure testifies to the arrival and development of the Itzá, and the advance
of their religious ideas. Its style is what we call "Maya-Yucatec", mixed with elements from the original populace —Puuc or Serranía. The building's architecture,
the sculpture and the painting, all pay homage to the military and religious cult to
Kukulcán which, towards the end of the Mesoamerican Classic Period had began to
spread into the Maya region, producing a cultural and social renaissance in Yucatán.

The Ball Court has a rectangular base 168 metres long and 70 metres wide
upon which is a central alley or court enclosed on the east and west sides by two
parallel platforms. The central court communicates with two lateral courts on the
north and south sides, boarded by walls so as to provide four entrances. Together,
this arrangement of structures forms an I shape, in common with other Ball
Courts in Mesoamerica.

The platforms, each 95 metres long, have large staircases with balustrades on
each side, which ascend to the upper part where there were three small, almost
square structures, perhaps temples or rooms for the priests, judges, players and nobles to watch the game. Each platform has a decorated border of panels in bas-
relief, one in the centre and one at each end and upon each rises a vertical wall face
8 metres in height, with a ring of stone in the centre, decorated with interlocking
plumed serpents to represent Kukulcán or Quetzalcóatl *(Figs. 20, 21, 23)*.

The central panels on the borders show a procession of warrior-players, seven
on each side of a central circular motif in the form of a skull, symbolising death.
The first figure of the right hand group is decapitated, and from his neck blood
stylised in the form of serpents runs out. He has one knee on the ground. The first
figure in the left hand group is a sacrificer, carrying a knife or dagger in one hand
and the head of the decapitated figure in the other *(Fig. 22)*.

All the figures are richly carved and decorated with magnificent feathered hea-
dresses on their helmets and backs. Many have earpieces that fasten behind the ear-
lobe and nose adornments made of clay, round arm shields like puffed sleeves, wide
belts in the shape of a yoke round their waists and "palmas" facing them. There are

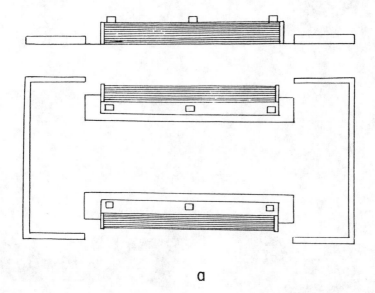

a

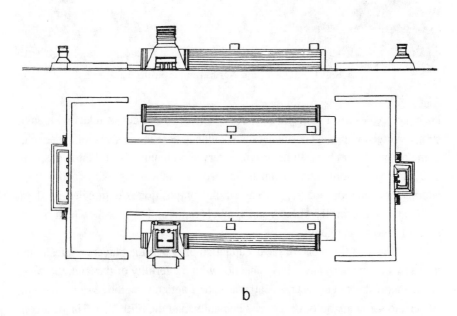

b

20. Plan of the Ball Court. a) Original base. b) Modification of the base by the
construction of the North and South Temples, and the Temple of the Tigers.

21. The Ball Court, with the North Temple in the background.

knee pieces, beautiful disks on the back of the belts and also sandals with ankle straps, skirted or aproned costumes and shoulder pieces in the shape of cut conchs. Some of the players have stone insignias carved with animals in their hands, butterfly shaped nose ornaments, helmets adorned with animal engravings and pectoral adornments made of jade pieces. The whole composition is completed by floral motifs, festoons, scrolls, volutes and symbols representing speech, which fill the spaces between the figures.

It is clear that the scene of the decapitation of one of the players relates to human sacrifice, perhaps having a connection with the fertility of the land, the water or the sun. Kukulcán or Quetzalcóatl was god of agriculture, the seasons, the year and creator of mankind or of the new humanity, and the Fifth Sun. This last concept was introduced by the Itzá, whose customs and cultural elements were adopted from other parts, as for example, the use of clay nose adornments, in the Huastec style or the pectoral with decorations symbolising the wind or Quetzalcóatl in the

22. (above). Detail of a central panel in the Ball Court, showing a scene of sacrifice. 23. View of the Ball Court with the stone ring. At one end is the Temple of the Tigers.

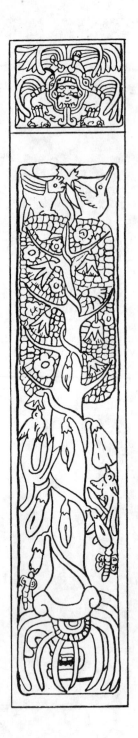

24. Drawing of the
balustrades that
border the staircase
of the North Temple.

shape of a cut conch, the belts-yokes, the "palmas" and the animal engraved stone insignia as well as the decapitation scenes where the blood runs out in the form of serpents, all originating in Aparicio, Veracruz. The scrolls and volutes pertained to groups from the centre of Veracruz at around the end of the Classic Period.

The Ball Court itself, with its panels decorated in bas-relief, is similar to the El Tajín style, Veracruz. The realistic serpents that finish off the panels at each of the ends symbolise Quetzalcóatl, whose cult originated in Xochicalco. All these examples, lead one to conclude that both the ideas and people who arrived in Chichén came because of the conquest of that place by the Itzá, who began to influence the society and culture of the original group of Maya that they found settled there.

North Temple or Temple of the Bearded Man

In this building, built after the Ball Court, one can see the influence of the Itzá and of their religious ideas. It adjoins the north wall which forms one side of the temple, and has a platform nearly 14 metres long and 8 metres wide. On top of this is a base in three parts, with inclining walls and a central staircase facing south. The staircase balustrades are decorated with trees, their roots buried in the "earthmonster". Leafy branches or creepers coil round the trunks, and there are butterflies and birds all around, some settled on the tops of the trees. Above the trees, in a separate square or panel, appears Quetzalcóatl or Kukulcán representing the man-bird-serpent, with a forked tongue and plumed body, his face emerging from the jaws of the serpent *(Fig. 24)*.

The temple, which is 10 metres long and 6 metres wide, rises from the podium. It consists of a single room, with a vaulted roof. The facade has a sloping wall face which finishes with a slightly projecting moulding. Then, there is a vertical wall up to the height of the lintels, which rest on two columns with bas-relief work. Above the lintels there is a plain border finished with a moulded cornice, and continuing above the border is a plain frieze, finished with another cornice, this time inverted and with a moulding.

This temple introduces a new architectural style: the sloping elevation and the vertical wall, which was common in Xochicalco, Morelos and was widely used in Chichén Itzá. Other elements are also notable, such as the columns decorated with bas-relief, the tall jambs decorated with warriors, the lower panel with the effigy of

25. View of the North Temple or the Temple of the Bearded Man.

the man-bird-serpent and the Maya vault totally decorated with a variety of every-day and religious scenes *(Figs. 25, 26, 27)*.

Thus, on one part of the back wall one contemplates a scene in which the deity Kukulcán appears seated on a jaguar-thone. This is surrounded by an oval shaped outline in the form of a plumed serpent. On either side of the god there are seven figures, mainly warriors with *átlatl* or slings, arrows and back disks on their belts. One of them seems to be the chief with a serpent design like an inverted S on his back. In the next row appears the Lord Kukulcán, priest and ruler. He has a tunic decorated with precious stones and chalchihuites (a precious green stone, supposed to come from the place of the same name in Zacatecas), and to his left are seven seated figures, all of whom have butterfly shaped pectoral decorations. On his right there are six other dignatories, also seated. Beneath them runs another row of dig-natories, seven on the left, two in the guise of eagles, and another seven on the right, two of these standing over the roof of a house or temple, in which there are two seated figures.

Finally, further down, there is a border showing the dead Lord and priest Ku-kulcán, his tunic finely inlaid with chalchihuites and a serpent with two heads coming out from his belt. One of the serpents heads is turned down towards his

26. Detail of the vault of the North temple with bas-reliefs.

27. Detail of a jamb from the North Temple, showing the representation of Kukulcán or Venus.

28. View of the South Temple.

feet and the other is turned upwards, as if protecting him. On each side of him are two seated individuals, one of whom appears to be coming out of a conch shell, that is surounded with intertwining leaf shapes.

All these scenes are related both to the Itzá and to Kukulcán. This can be seen in the representation of the god, who appears in the upper part or sky, and the lord-priest who carries the same name as the warriors, nobles and priests upon whom he depends for support and allegiance. On his death the lord-priest descends to the underworld in the custody of the deity and the gods of the four corners of the world, perhaps the Bacabes or Pauahtunes. The clothing of the figures is the same as those on the Ball Court: puffed sleeves, clay nose adornments, back disks on the belts, plumed headdresses, eagle or bird disguises and butterfly shaped pectorals. The temple also displays leafy scrolls and volutes, in a slightly more emphasised style, and the jaguar throne and serpents symbolised by the inverted S shape.

The South Temple

This structure was built after the Ball Court, as a platform was built up against the south wall of the Court which enclosed it. This building has a rectangular platform 25 metres long and 8 metres wide. It also has a sloping wall with a light moulding, a vertical wall, a raised border or panel, a moulded cornice, a frieze and finishing with an inverted cornice. There are seven entrances, formed by six pillars decorated with figures of warriors and covered with hieroglyphs that indicate their names. On the base there are panels with the effigy of the man-bird-serpent or Kukulcán, coming out of the jaws of the plumed serpent. *(Fig. 28)*

Temple of the Tigers

In order to build this structure it was necessary to cut the large stairway from the eastern platform of the Ball Court, and also to demolish the small structure at the southern end. This all occurred after the construction of the North and South Temples already described. A pyramid shaped foundation was constructed with a narrow staircase reaching the level of the platform on the south side, which was 10 metres in height.

On top of the podium a low platform was built with a stairway. The stairway balustrades are decorated with reliefs aluding to Kukulcán, who is facing west. On this platform rests the temple, which is almost square based, with two parallel chambers, each with two rooms. One of these funcions as a vestibule and the other as a sanctuary. The facade has a sloping elevation and a plain, vertical wall, a slightly raised border and a frieze in between two moulded panels totally decorated in bas-relief on a stone mosaic base. According to Stephens:

> The door opens upon the platform of the wall, overlooking the Tennis-court [Ball Court]. The front corridor was supported by massive pillars, portions of which still remain, covered with elaborate sculptured ornaments. The lintel of the inner doorway is a beam of sapote [chewing gum tree], richly carved. The jambs are partly buried in the rubble.... [and in] an inner chamber, the walls and ceiling of which are covered, from the floor to the peak of the arch, with designs in painting, representing, in bright and vivid colours, human figures, battles, houses, trees and scenes of domestic life...

The first room or vestibule has three doorways formed by two serpentine columns. The serpents heads form the base and the tails the capitals supporting the lintels. The door jambs are decorated with warriors. Inside the vestibule are the remains of painted frescos and amongst these is a battle scene which takes place near a village with huts probably made from palm, which is set on fire after being conquered *(Figs. 29, 30, 31)*.

The building's frieze, which gave it its name, has a lower panel consisting of

29. (above) The Temple of the Tigers, on the east platform of the Ball Court.
30. Detail of a serpentine column in the same temple.

31. Facade of the Temple of the Tigers, showing serpentine columns.

32. Temple of the Tigers: detail of the frieze, with jaguars, shields, intertwined serpents and other motifs.

two mouldings with interlocking serpents, leaving a central border decorated with two jaguars on each end, and with two on the centre of the principal entrance. The jaguars are all walking in opposite directions towards three interlocking warriors shields. On the upper panel are two plumed serpents. The serpents heads are at either end of the panel and their tails meet in the centre. Engaged balusters or drums are set into the undulations of the snake's body and the panel is finished by a moulding of interlocking serpents, and a crown with a series of circular shields, each crossed with two arrows *(Fig. 32)*.

So as to further develop the cult to Kukulcán, on the back of the building and along the edge of the platform, are two realistic serpents that commence in the centre and whose heads come out on each of the extremes. Both here and on the sides of the temple, there are sunken and undecorated panels on the vertical elevation.

The Annex of the Tigres

This building was built some time after the Temple of the Tigres and adjoins the base of the earlier temple at the level of the exterior plaza. The new temple consists of a single room with a vaulted roof, in keeping with the new style introduced by the Itzá. Accordingly, this structure displays a sloping elevation or embankment, a vertical wall and a frieze in between two cornice mouldings. The front walls of the building are decorated with warriors and panels showing the man-bird-serpent. There are also three door openings formed by two square pillars, also with figures of warriors, and panels representing Kukulcán as lord of the earth and of vegetation.

The interior of the temple is also decorated. There are rows of warriors carrying *átlatl* and darts, wearing plumed headdresses, butterfly shaped pectorals, belts with back disks and puffed sleeves or knee pieces. In this scene is also a seated figure on a jaguar throne, similar to that between the two square pillars of the building. There is also a warrior chief and in the background a plumed serpent in an S shape. The rest of the composition is filled with scrolls, volutes and spirals, some leafy, but all in a much more caligraphic style suggesting that, at this juncture, the Itzá artists are losing their original sense of style and design *(Figs. 33, 34, 35, 36)*.

Substructure of the Castle

This is a building formed by a podium consisiting of nine stepped structures, whose original height was 16 metres. It had a single stairway facing to the north. On top of the podium is a temple with two parallel chambers and vaulted roofs. The first chamber serves as a vestibule and the second as a sanctuary, and both of them have only one entrance. The temple's facade has a plain vertical section and a frieze in between two cornice mouldings. The frieze's central border is divided by two intertwined serpents and a procession of jaguars on each side, running in opposite directions. There are war shields on the upper section. The cornice has a border of toothed bars forming inverted triangles simulating a broken serpent.

Inside the vestibule is a chacmool, with eyes, teeth and nails inlaid in bone. Inside the sanctuary is a jaguar throne painted in red, and the jaguar's skin is marked with spots in circles of jade. The fangs are worked in flint. The throne is decorated with a disk made of a mosaic of turquoise, and with four serpentine motifs worked in shell. On the base of the staircase a box containing the offering of the building has been found, which contains wooden disks with mosaics of turquoise, coral and shell and also sacrificial knives. There are jade panels engraved with figures, necklaces and other objects.

33. Location of the Annex of the Tigers on the rear wall of the Temple of the Tigers.

34. Front view of the Annex of the Tigers.

35. Throne in the form of a jaguar and mask of the god Kukulcán in the Annex of the Tigers.

36. Drawing of a warrior found on one of the inner walls of the annex of the Tigers.

The Temple of Chacmool or Substructure of the Warriors

This constructuion has a podium 24 metres long with three sections of sloping or inclined walls, decorated with raised rectangles that leave equally spaced sunken sections. It is crowned with a projecting band. On the west side is a balustraded staircase providing access to the temple.

The temple is 18 metres long with two parallel chambers. The first is a vestibule with two square, serpentine pillars forming three door openings. These are painted in bright colours and with figures of priests. There are also four internal square pillars. The second chamber or sanctuary has a single opening and four more square pillars supporting roof beams.

In the interior of the sanctuary there are benches against the walls, an altar and paintings on the walls, representing rows of dignatories both sitting and standing. Some of these carry sceptres in their hands. Others are lords on thrones, with feather adornments, helmets and darts in their hands. There is also a chacmool which ought to be situated at the front of the main entrance, who wears a type of helmet or hat decorated with a frog, and from each side of his belt hang small human heads, perhaps related to the decapitation rituals. The square pillars would once have had stucco work and would have been painted with lords and priests with masks and elaborate clothing.

The Northeastern Colonnade. Originally the front of the Temple of Chacmool had a portico perhaps consisting of three rows of square pillars, possibly thirty in number, set on a low platform with a staircase on the west side. Later, when the Temple of the Warriors was built, with its much larger dimensions, a fourth row of pillars was added to the former three, and others on the north and south sides, so that in total there were some 63 pillars, much as can be seen today. In order to accomplish the extension it was also necessary to extend the supporting platform, and its corresponding flight of three steps. Two pillars were suspended or inserted into each of the altar-benches flanking the stairway to the Temple of the Warriors, and another two pillars were removed and replaced on two former ones. In this way part of the stairway of that temple was formed, now at a greater height, and roofing nearly a third of the staircase.

The name "Northeast Colonnade" is not really appropriate to the building as these are not cylindrical columns but rather square pillars. Furthermore, they are located on the west side of the Temple of the Warriors and of its Substructure or

37. Detail of the
Northeast Colonnade.

Temple of Chacmool. All of the pillars are decorated on each of the four faces with reliefs of warriors and sometimes of priests, as well as with panels carrying effigies of the man-bird-serpent, or Kukulcán *(Fig. 37)*.

The Caracol

This building consists of a rectangular platform measuring 67 metres from north to south and 52 metres from east to west. It has a single, slightly sloping structure with a cornice with rounded corners, whose total height is 6 metres. On the west front there is a staircase, rising up in three steps from a low platform, which is borded by narrow balustrades decorated with intertwined serpents.

On top of this platform there was a circular base, 11 metres in diameter and 3.70 metres high. This was a single vertical structure between two cornice mouldings. Another base was built on top of this one, 16 metres in diameter and 5 metres high. The new base was a single structure with sloping banks and a projecting moulding, and above a vertical wall finished with another moulding. Later, a rectangular terrace was added to the front, 20 metres long and 6.50 metres wide. This had a vertical elevation finished with a slightly projecting moulding. Finally, all was covered by a terrace, of a rectangular but irregular base, 24 metres across at its widest point. It had a vertical wall and a wide band to finish. The stairway on the west side is boarded by balustrades decorated with intertwined serpents *(Fig. 38)*.

From this terrace one observes the circular based tower set directly on top of the first platform, 11 metres in diameter. The first member of the tower is formed by two concentric walls which contain two ring shaped chambers, with vaulted roofs. Each of them has four doors and a central nucleus where there is a small spiral staircase. The exterior of the structure is a plain, vertical wall and a cornice with a wide moulding, reaching a height of 4.50 metres.

The second member is contained within the cornice of the former and another narrower cornice also with a moulding. Above each of the doors is a frieze with a mask of Chac, and a seated figure incised with plumed and serpent motifs. The third member is now largely destroyed, but shows a series of small openings or windows, that perhaps relate to astronomical observations, thus leading to the building also being known as The Observatory.

The total height of the tower is 13 metres and the total height of the monument is 22.50 metres. If we take into account that the tower is set directly onto the first platform of 11 metres in diameter, it is not improbable that this originally would only have had the central nucleus with the spiral stair that leads up to the third member or observatory, surrounded by the circular chamber of the first member. Later, when the other two platforms to the building were added, they would have extended the building with the construction of the other circular chamber. The terrace that today can be seen surrounding the whole tower was built last of all *(Figs. 39, 40, 41)*.

Other buildings

The structures briefly described correspond to the times when the Itzá governed under the alliance or League of Mayapán. The Itzá introduced the cult to Kukulcán or Quetzalcóatl (originally as a Venus deity, creator of the Fifth Sun and of the new man kind), iniciating and developing an architectural and artistic style that we have called Maya-Yucatec. This style was a combination of elements from several other regions and based on the foundations of the Puuc-Chen tradition that prevailed in the area. This new style is concentrated particularly in the north of the site, near to

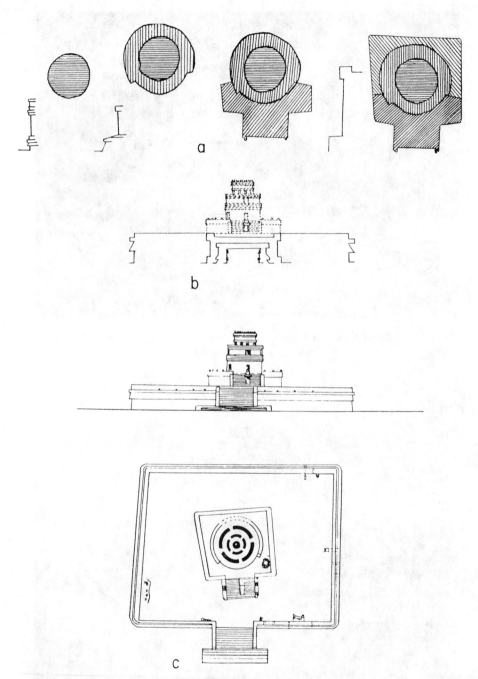

38. Plan of the Caracol. a) Floor plans of the bases for inner support b) Location of the bases. c) The building in the final building stage.

39. (above). The Caracol, or Observatory, in the time of Stephens. 40. The present day building viewed from the Church.

41. Detail of the circular structures of the Observatory.

42. Temple of the Lintel, in Old Chichén.

43. Temple of the Four Lintels: lintel with relief showing Kukulcán coming out of the jaws of a serpent with the body of a bird.

the Sacred Cenote, or Sacrificial Well, although due to the vastness of the city, and as an illustration of their dominion over their subjects, there are other buildings by the Itzá inside the old complexes or adjoining earlier structures.

For example, on the back side of the base or building of the Chichanchob, a small Ball Court was built which had a band decorated with reliefs of player-warriors. In Old Chichén there is a building known as the Temple of the Four Lintels. One of the lintels displays the figure of Kukulcán coming out of the fangs of a realistic serpent. Also in Old Chichén is the Temple of the Lintel, so called because of an old stone lintel that was re-used and relocated over the top of the two columns *(Figs. 42, 43)*.

THE SECOND PERIOD OF THE MILITARY CITY

The alliance forged between the three cities of Chichén Itzá, Uxmal and Mayapán (The League of Mayapán) enabled the Itzá to maintain friendly relations with the tribes of these cities, the Xiu and Cocom. The league was formed in 1185 and lasted until 1204 A. D., finally breaking up when a Lord of Mayapán, Hunac Ceel, conquered Chichén. With this conquest he increased his power and achieved the hegemony of Mayapán. In referrence to this *Chilam Balam de Chumayel* says:

> The only true God is our Lord Dios; they worshipped him according to the word and the wisdom of Mayapán. Ah Kin Cobá was their priest there in the fortress <of Mayapán>. Zulim Chan was at the west <gate>. Nauat...in the south gate. Couoh [and Ah Canul] was the guardian of the east gate. Ah Ek was his companion. This was their ruler: Ah Tapay Nok Cauich was the name of their head chief; Hunac Ceel was the representative of Ah Mex Cuc.
> Then he demanded one complete Plumeria flower [a whole flower]. Then he demanded a white mat. Then he demanded a mantle faced on two sides [two dresses]. Then he demanded a green turkey [blue turkey]. [then he demanded his lassoo for hunting] Then he demanded a mottled snail. Then he demanded the gourds called homa [white earthenware vessels].

Thus, within the walled city of Mayapán the priest was Ah Kin Cobá, the guardian of the west gate was Tzulim Chan and of the south gate Nauat. Couoh and Ah Canul guarded the east gate and Ah Ek the north. The lord was Ah Tapai Nok and the *halach uinic* or governor was Hunac Ceel Cauich, who also was servant and priest to Ah Mex Cuc (of the squirrel's beard). This deity was conceived of as Kukulcán but had solar functions rather than ones related to Venus. It is possible that he was god of fire, warfare and the sun.

Hunac Ceel held absolute power over a vast region and a single throne (symbolised by a Plumeria flower and a white mat). His domain included two lordships (señorios, in Spanish) that of Mayapán and of Chichén Itzá (the mantle faced on two sides [or two dresses]) and great riches (green [or blue] turkey, mottled snails, gourds [or earthenware vessels for balché]). He finally succeeded in breaking the existing union or league, by attacking and conquering Chichén. According to the *Crónica Matichu:*

8 Ahau (1185-1204) it was in Chichén Itzá, mouth of the well. It then happened that the Lord of Uxmal was painted and came to leave his footprint on the back of Chac Xib Chac, [red-terrible-Chac] in Chichén [mouth of the well], where Ah Nacxit Kukulcán [the Nacxit-serpent-quetzal] reigned; then it was that the success of the Itzá [wise men of the water] decreased and there came a time of grim fighting, of fierce fighting, of violent fighting, of fighting without pity.

Sin came, in 8 Ahau. It came and it weakened the Ceiba (indigenous tree) because of Ah Xib Chac, [the terrible Chac] of Chichén...

It was in 8 Ahau that the Ah Ulil [the snail] episode happened in Itzamal [place of the wise men of the water], when the Lord Ah Ulil was defeated and beaten... for the sin committed with the woman of his friend, another Lord. This caused the war...

[there in Izamal or Itzmal]... they paid a tribute with the children of Itzmal Kauil [holy place of the wise men of the water] to feed the Hapai Can [swallowing snake] who made violent war. Then it was in Itzmal... it occurred during the reign of Lord Ulil... that the power of Hapai Can ended...that had the ones of Itzmal Thul...

Great was the suffering for those of Ah Itzmal Thul [the wise men of the rushing water], great was the sorrow of his soul. Beaten and bound was Ahau Canul [lord, prince, guardian] for his sins, because he presented the children as tribute to Hapai Can... Because of this he was dominated by Ah Kukulcán [serpent-quetzal] so that all the inhabitants of Itzmal Thul should bear witness.

A synthesized version of this quotation could be interpreted in the following way. Around 1185-1204 the Cocom of Mayapán declared war on Chichén Itzá at which time they also rebelled against Uxmal [painting of the lord]. They went to conquer Chichén and initiated the fighting. The lord there was Chac Xib Chac [settle on his back] and the cult to Nac-xit-Kukulcán reigned. They also declared war in Izamal, whose lord Ulil used to make child sacrifices to Hapai Can or the swallowing snake [original symbol of Kukulcán], which resulted in his downfall.

In relation to the above, it is necessary to recall that Hunac Ceel of Mayapán was the servant of Ah Mex Cuc [he of the squirrel's beard], which perhaps was a dedicatory title for Kukulcán as god of the solar fires and of the war. It must be remembered that in Mayapán they also worshipped Kukulcán as he founded that city after Chichén. In Chichén and Izamal at this time they worshipped Nacxit Kukulcán. As a result of this war the ancient cult to Kukulcán [based on Hapai Can or the swallowing snake] was displaced, and another title or image was imposed on him signifying sun, fire, war [in Izamal, Kinich Kakmó; in Chichén, Ah Mex Cuc]. This may be because the ancient high priests [kukulcanes] had died and then were deified with different names [Ah Nacxit Kukulcán, Ah Kukulcán, Ah Mex Cuc]. According to the *Crónica Matichu:*

> The tenth tun 8 Ahau [1194], was the year when they dispersed because of Ah Sinteut Chan, Tzontecum, Taxcal, Pantemit, Xuchueuet, Itzcuat, Cacaltecat. These were the names of the individuals, seven from Mayapán.
>
> In the same 8 Ahau they [from Mayapán] went to destroy King Ulmil, because of his feasts with the King Ulil of Itzmal [1185-1204].
>
> Thirteen katun folds the Itzá had been established when they   dispersed because of Hunac Ceel, who taught a lesson to the   Itzá [987-1007 to 1224-1244].

Thus, around 1185-1204 A. D. Hunac Ceel of Mayapán commenced the conquest of Chichén Itzá. He defeated Chac-Xib Chac, lord of Chichén, with the help of seven captains from Mayapán [of Nahua origin]. He also fought against the people of Izamal [Itzmal], who perhaps were allied to Chichén. The governor of Chichén Itzá was forced to abandon the site in the company of some of the Itzá, around 1204-1244 A. D.

It appears that Hunac Ceel was not well received by the people of Chichén Itzá. He was a conqueror and not a lord elected by the principals. As such, he had to be submitted to a test which involved throwing himself into the *cenote* or holy well, to see if the gods of the water would give their consent.

It is described in the *Chilam Balam de Chumayel*:

> It was Cauich, Hunac Ceel, Cauich was the name of the man there, who put his head at the opening of the well on the south side. Then he went to take it. Then he came forth to declare the prophecy. Then began the taking of the proohecy. Then began his prophecy. Then they began to declare him ruler. The he was set in the seat of the rulers by them.
>
> Then they began to declare him head chief. He was not the ruler formerly; that was the office of Ah Mex Cuc. Now the representative of Ah Mex Cuc was decalred ruler. The eagle they say was his mother. Then they say he was sought on his hill. Then they began to take the prophecy of this ruler after it was declared.
>
> Then they began to set aloft the house on high for the ruler. Then began the construction of the stairway. Then he was set in the house on high in 13 Ahau, the sixth reign. Then began the hearing of the prophecy, of the news, of the setting up of Ah Mex Cuc as he was called.

Hunac Ceel submitted himself to the test of being hurled into the cenote or

well, from the south side, emerging on the surface of the water. This feat permitted him to demand that he be treated as Lord (Ahau), almost as a god. The almost
deified position may also be as a result of having introduced the cult of Ah Mex-
Cuc [of the squirrel's beard], itself perhaps a variation of Kukulcán as the man
with the squirrel beard and solar god, deity to whom he was servant or priest and
who occupied his place in the thirteen heavens, between the thirteen lords. According to his status, they built the High House and the stone staircase, or Castle (El
Castillo) which obstructs the original building.

When Chichén was conquered by Hunac Ceel several of the Itzá abandonded the
site causing an exodus that possibly corresponds to the "Little Descent" from the
east. They passed though different outposts and places before settling on the outskirts of Mayapán.

Thus, in *Chilam Balam de Chumayel*, although perhaps in exaggerated form, it
states:

> Thirteen katuns they ruled, and then came the treachery of Hunac Ceel. Their
> town was abandoned and they went into the heart of the forest to Tanxulucmul,
> as it is called...
>
> Whereupon they departed and arrived at Ppolé, where the remainder of the Itzá
> were increased in number; they took the women of Ppole as their mothers. Then
> they arrived at Aké; there they were born at Aké.... Then they arrived at Chikin-
> dzonot... Then they arrived at Xppitah (Espita)... Then they came to Timaax,
> where they made complete rogues of themselves.
>
> Then they arrived at Buctzotz... Then they arrived at Dzidzuntun... Then they
> arrived at the town of Chac... Then they arrived at Baca... Then they went to
> Ixil... Then they came to Itzamna (Itzimná). Then they came to Chubulná. Then
> they arrived at Caucel... Then they went to Hunucmá... Then they arrived at Ux-
> mal... Then they arrived at Munaa... Then they arrived at Dzam... Then they
> went to Ticul... Then they went to Uman and to Ichcanzihoo... And the [great]
> Mayapán, the fortress [on the water].

Thus, when the Itzá abandoned Chichén in 1204-1244 A. D. they went to Polé,
a port near to Tulum, in the east. They passed by Aké, Tizimin (Chikin-dzonot),
Espita (Xppitah), Temax (Ti-maax), Buctzotz, Dzinzntún, Telchac (Chac), Baca,
Ixil, Itimná, Chuburná, Caucel, Hunucmá, Uxmal, Muna Ticul, Umán, Mérida
(Ich- caan-sihó) and Mayapán, and numerous other places indicated in the sources.
The Chumayel, or the Balam who dictated to them, exaggerated the abandonment
of Chichén and described it as an exodus or migration: they went east, north, west
and south in Yucatán before reaching Mayapán, where they were defeated.

However, the *Chilam Balam de Chumayel* continues:

4 Ahau was when the land of Ich-paa Mayapán was siezed [conquered] by the Itzá men who had been separated from their homes because of the people of Izamal and because of the treachery of Hunac Ceel.

And the *Cronica Matichu:*

4 Ahau. Was when the land of Ichpá-Mayapán was seized by the men of Itzá who had left their homes with the Kink Ulil, and because of the people of Itzmal, because of the treachery of Hunac Ceel.

Thus, both the Itzá and the Itzamaleños reached Mayapán and settled outside the walls of the city, as can be seen in Landa:

On the departure of Cuculcán the chiefs agreed that for the permanence of the state the house of the Cocoms should exercise the chief authority, it being the oldest and richest, or perhaps because its head was at that time a man of greater power. This done they ordained that... they should build outside the walls dwellings where each of them might keep some serving people, and whither the people from the villages might come whenever they had business at the city. In these houses each one placed his mayordomo...

The people that abandoned Chichén Itzá went to Mayapán where they occupied the sector that had been assigned to them during the period of the League or alliance, in the same way as the people of Izamal. With the conquest of both Chichén Itzá and Izamal the people of Mayapán exercised their power over the vast region. Due to inevitable uprisings they dominated a number of towns and lordships (señoríos). Even in Mayapán itself, there was a conflict between those who lived outside the city walls and those who lived within.

In the *Cronica de Matichu* it says:

11 Ahau [1283-1303] The land of Ichpá-Mayapán was siezed by those outside the walls, because of the multiple government inside the walls of Mayapán, by the men of Itzá and the King Ulmil.

But it is not until several years later that Mayapán was conquered and destroyed. In the Cronica Matichu it says:

8 Ahau [1441-1461]. Was the year when Ichpá-Mayapán was abandoned and de-

stroyed by those from outside the walls, those on the other side of the walls, because of the multiple government in the interior of Mayapán.

And in the *Chilam Balam de Chumayel* it is written:

8 Ahau was when there was fighting with stones at Ich-paa Mayapán because of the seizure of the fortress. They broke down the city wall because of the joint government in Mayapán.

The Itzá who remained in Chichén under the domination of the people of Mayapán continued to develop their own culture, as can be seen in the architecture and artistic works. There are, however, traces of Mexican or later elements, due to the involvement of mercenaries contracted by the Cocoms to fight their wars, just before the fall of Mayapán. Roughly between 1185 and 1350 buildings such as The Castle (El Castillo), The Temple of the Warriors (El Templo de los Guerreros), The Temple of the Eagles and Tigers (El Templo de las Aguilas y Tigres), The Temple of Venus (El Templo de Venus), The Temple of a Thousand Columns (El Templo de Las Mil Columnas), The Market (El Mercado), The Wall of Skulls (El Tzompantli), and others were constructed.

During these years elements such as painted murals recording or commemorating the war and conquest of Mayapán by the Cocom were added. Amongst other additions and adornments were the painted gourds, gold and copper disks decorated with war scenes, reliefs of eagles and jaguars eating human hearts, small temples or mausoleums with a flight of four steps, altars of skulls, decorated benches and castellations finishing off the roofs of the buildings.

The Castle

For the celebrated traveller Stephens, the Castle was:

From every point of view the grandest and most conspicuous object that towers above the plain... on the ground at the foot of the staircase, forming a bold, striking and well conceived commencement to this lofty range, are two colossal serpents' heads, ten feet in length, with mouths wide open and tongues protruding... No doubt they were emblematic of some religious belief... [and the temple has] single doorways [that] face east, south and west, having massive lintels of *zapote* wood covered with elaborate carvings, and the jambs are ornamented with sculptured figures... The doorway facing to the north... presents a grander ap-

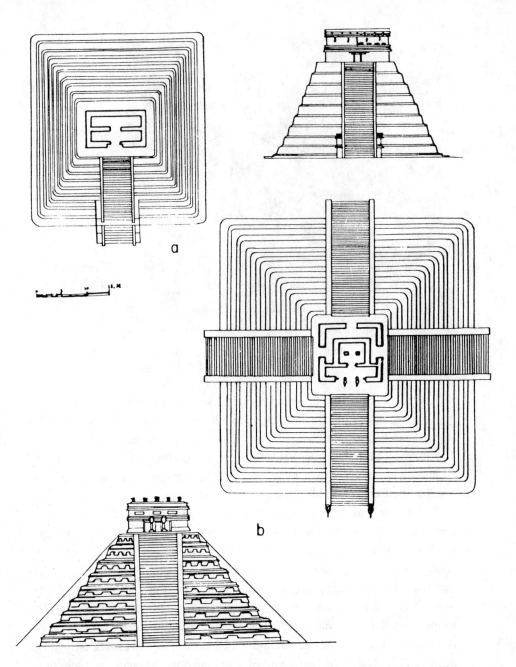

44. Plan of the Castle. a) Substructure with single staircase. b) The Castle which covered the earlier structure.

45. Head of a plumed serpent at the foot of one of the balustrades of the Castle.

pearance... having two, short, massive columns... [and in the sanctuary] are two square pillars... having sculptured figures on all their sides...

This construction is composed of a square base 55.5 metres each side. There are nine sloping, stepped sections which reach a height of 24 metres, decorated with slightly raised rectangles that give the impression of cape-shaped panels in the Zapotec or El Tajin style from Veracruz. Access to the temple is by four balustraded stairways, one on each side of the base. The northern staircase conserves its colossal plumed serpents heads at the base *(Figs. 44, 45)*.

The temple consists of a vestibule with three entrances formed by two serpentine columns. The heads form the bases of the columns and the tails form the capitals to support the wooden lintels. From the vestibule one passes on to the sanctuary or vaulted chamber which has two square pillars decorated in bas- relief. These sustain the horizontal support beams of the roof. Behind this chamber runs a narrow gallery with three doors opening on to the west, south and east staircases. The temple has a sloping elevation and a plain, vertical wall. Above is a frieze between two cornice mouldings, whose central border has three sunken panels, one with a mask of Chac, god of the rain, on a level with the principal entrance. The roof is finished with castellations, in the form of cut conch shells or symbols of the wind. The jambs and the inner pillars display warriors and other richly decorated figures *(Figs. 46, 47, 48)*.

47. North view of the Castle. 48. The same building in the time of Stephens.

The Temple of the Warriors

This building consists of a quadrangular base that measures 40 metres on each side. It has stepped sections, composed of sloping elevations and cornice-panels, these last decorated in bas-relief showing warriors, eagles and jaguars devouring human hearts, and also the figure of Kukulcán or Venus in the form of Tlalchiton-atiuh. The staircase, which faces west, is balustraded. The balustrades are decorated

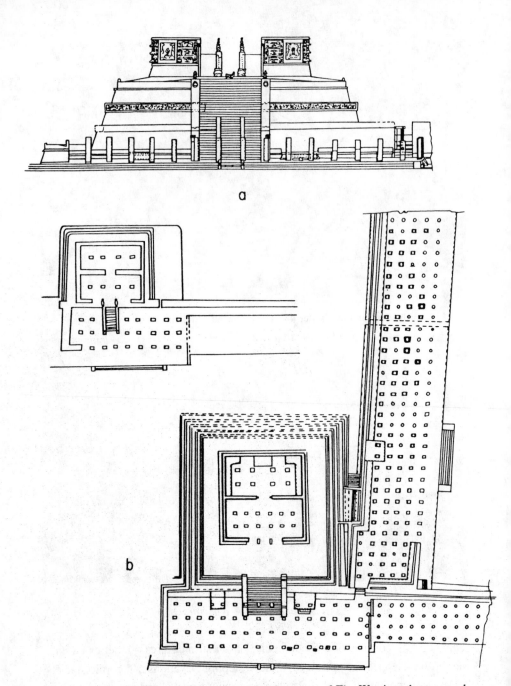

49. Plan of The Warriors. a) Substructure. b). Structure of The Warriors that covered the previous one, together with the Northeast Colonnade and the Thousand Columns.

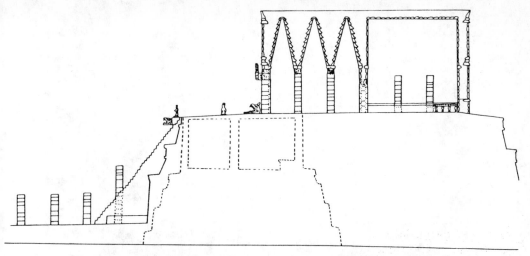

50. Cross-section of the Temple of the Warriors showing the substructure.

in bas-relief with plumed serpents, whose heads now dominate the upper dado where the standard bearers, sculptured in the form of warriors would have been set *(Figs. 49, 50, 51)*.

On top of the base is the almost square shaped temple, 21 metres on each side, leaving an ample platform to the front. It has two parallel chambers. The first, has three entrances formed by two, very slender serpentine pillars, with twelve square pillars in the interior supporting the horizontal beams of the roof. The beams are decorated with figures of gods and warriors, and have minor panels carrying the effigie of Kukulcán. The second chamber, or sanctuary, has a single entrance, eight square pillars and a stone altar against the back wall, sustained by Atlantes in the form of warriors *(Figs. 52, 53)*.

The temple's facade is composed of a sloping elevation and a vertical wall, which really functions as a frieze. It is interrupted by the main entrance, and decorated on each side with a plaque, three superimposed masks of Chac (one with the effigie of the god Kukulcán coming out of the jaws of the plumed serpent, with

51. Standard bearer at the head of one of the balustrades of the Temple of the Warriors.

52. Altar sustained by atlantes in the sanctuary of the Temple of the Warriors.

53. General view of the Temple of the Warriors.

54. (above left). Entrance to the Temple of the Warriors with square, serpentine pillars. 55. (above right). Entrance to the same Temple with a Chacmool in the foreground. 56. Detail of Chacmool.

forked tongue), and another three masks of Chac on the corner, one on top of the other, each with the characteristic curved and protruding noses. Above this frieze is another plain frieze between two cornice mouldings. The temple was completed with castellations on the roof, of which none remain. On the platform and in front of the main entrance there is a well proportioned Chacmool *(Figs. 54. 55. 56)*.

The Thousand Columns Group

This grouping refers to a vast square or plaza in the form of an irregular quadrangle, of some 150 metres on each side. There are some constructions on the east and south sides, amongst them the so called Market, which complete the square on these sides. On the west side is a colonnade of four rows of columns with stone drums and capitals. Above the capitals, sit the beams sustaining the vaulting, which run towards the north passing through the Portico of the Temple of the Warriors. On the northern side is another portico with five rows of columns set on a platform 2.20 metres high. This group is later than the buildings already described *(Figs. 57, 58)*.

The Market

This structure consists of a platform 80 metres long and 15 metres wide, with a central balustraded stairway giving access to a portico, open to the front and closed to the back and sides, with a row of alternating columns and square pillars sustaining the vaulted ceiling. A central door leads to a square patio, 17 metres on each side, surrounded by columns built with stone drums and capitals *(Fig. 59)*.

The facade of the portico has a sloping elevation and a vertical wall, divided by a horizontal band at the level of the supporting roof beams. Above the band is a frieze between two cornice mouldings, whose central border would have been decorated with groups of fluted columns. The facade is completed with castellations of cut conch-shells. Near to the central door of the portico is an adjoining platform with a moulding decorated with plumed serpents, and a sloping elevation showing a procession of warriors. Also, lying against the walls runs a bench with an inclined back.

57. The Thousand Columns in the time of Stephens.

58. Part of the Thousand Columns, viewed from the east.

59. Detail of the square pillars of the vestibule of The Market.

The Temple of Venus

This building has a square base of more than 25 metres on each side, with four balustraded stairways, all finishing in a dado or dado rail from which projects the head of a serpent whose body runs the length of the panel. The base has a sloping elevation, a band or vertical wall with raised panels that leave a sunken type space, and a panel-cornice to finish. The total height of the base is 4 metres.

On the raised panels there are bas-relief representations of the planet Venus, taking the form of the year symbol together with a half flower, engraved with crosses on the petals. There is also the symbol of Pop or a plaited mat which signifies lordship [señorío] or power. In the sunken spaces Kukulcán or Venus with forked tongue and jaguar-like claws appears coming out of the jaws of the plumed serpent. On the cornice is a plumed serpent, with fishes in the undulations of the body. The head of the serpent projects out from the dado rail of the balustrade *(Figs. 60, 61)*.

The decoration alluding to Venus or Kukulcán lent its name to the building. The temple is also known as the Tomb of Chacmool, in reference to a sculpture of this figure found in the interior by Le Plongeon. The sculpture is now to be seen in the National Museum of Anthropology.

Temple of the Eagles and Tigers

Another square based temple, this one also has four balustraded stairways. These are decorated with the bodies of plumed serpents which change from the vertical to the horizontal dimension to form a square block in the upper part of the balstrade where the four heads emerge. It is probable that there were jaguar-shaped standard bearers above the serpents' heads, displaying spotted jaguar skins similar to those found in the Sacred Cenote.

The base or platform has a sloping elevation, a band or vertical wall with raised panels and a cornice to finish. On the raised panels are reliefs of eagles eating human hearts and in the sunken spaces are beautiful representations of sitting jaguars with skins covererd with spots, as if scattered like flowers. They also are devouring human hearts. Kukulcán or Venus appears on the cornice in the form of a recumbent warrior wearing eyeglasses and with a lance in his hand. He is connected to Tlalchitonatiuh *(Figs. 62, 63, 64, 65)*.

The Annex to the Caracol

In the southeastern corner of the great platform of the Caracol or Observatory a rectangular platfrom was built on, with a balustraded stairway decorated with

60. Temple of Venus.

61. Detail of the Temple of Venus.

62. Temple of the Eagles and Tigers.

63. Detail of the Temple of the Eagles and the Tigers, with the Castle in the
background.

64. (left) Reliefs of Tlalchitonatiuh, an eagle and a jaguar in the Temple of the Eagles and Tigers. 65. Eagle devouring a human heart, in the same Temple.

66. View of the Caracol and its Annex.

67. (left). The Atlantes in the time of Stephens. 68. Temple of the Atlantes in
Old Chichén.

plumed serpents. On top of the platform was a temple or habitation 14 metres
long and 9 metres wide, consisting of two parallel chambers. The first served as a
vestibule with porticos formed by two rows of columns with capitals. The second
is a narrower chamber with a single doorway. Inside is a bench which occupies almost all the space. The facade of the building has a sloping elevation, a vertical
wall and a moulded cornice, all without decoration *(Fig. 66)*.

The Temple of the Atlantes

This temple is to be found in Old Chichén. It is a small building with masonry
walls, which have two large atlantes or caryatids in the front. These each represent
warriors, their hands raised up high so as to support the wooden lintels. These in
turn support the roof. The Atlantes are decorated with clay nose adornments, ear
decorations, wrist ornaments, pectorals, skirts, belts and sandals with heel pieces
(Figs. 67, 68, 69).

69. Detail of an
Atlante.

70. The Tzompantli.

The Tzompantli (Wall of Skulls)

This is a huge rectangular platform some 60 metres long and 12 metres wide, with a protrusion in the centre that gives it a T shape. The platform has a low, sloping elevation and a plaque formed by two mouldings and a central band decorated with three horizontal rows of skulls. It is supposed that on this platform there would have been a palisade on which to spike the heads of the sacrificed victims. The projecting section displays representations of eagles, and warriors carrying human heads in their hands. From here a Chacmool that had been burried in the platform was excavated *(Figs. 70, 71)*.

The Sacred Cenote

According to Diego de Landa, The Castle:

> had four stairways, and, in front of the north stairway, at some distance, there were two small theatres of masonry, with four staircases, and paved on top with stones, on which they presented plays and comedies to divert the people. From the court in front of these theatres there goes a beautiful broad paved way, leading to a well two stone-thows across. Into this well they were and still are accostomed to throw men alive as a sacrifice to the gods in times of drought; they held that they did not die, even though they were not seen again.
>
> They also threw in many other offerings of precious stones and things they

71. Detail of the skulls decorating the Tzompantli.

valued greatly; so if there were gold in this country, this well would have received most of it, so devout were the indians in this.

This well is seven long fathoms deep to the surface of the water, more than a
hundred feet wide, round, of natural rock marvellously smooth down to the water... At the top near the mouth, is a small building where I found idols made in
honour of all the principal buildings in the land, like the Pantheon at Rome... I
found sculptured lions, vases and other things, so that I do not understand how
anyone can asay that these people had no tools.

For his part, Stephens contributes the following:

Setting out from the Castle, at some distance we ascended a wooded elevation,
which seemed an artificial causeway leading to the senote. The senote was the
largest and wildest we had seen; in the midst of a thick forest, an immense, circular hole, with cragged, perpendicular sides, trees growing out of them and
overhanging the brink, and still as if the genius of silence reigned within... The
water was of a greenish hue [A misterious influence seemed to pervade it, in uni-
son with] the historical account that the well of Chichén was a place of pilgramage, and that human victims were thrown into it in sacrifice. In one place, on
the very brink, were the remains of a stone structure... perhaps the place from
which the victims were thrown into the dark well beneath.

In actual fact, the so called Sacred Cenote is a well of 50 metres in diameter
from north to south and 60.50 from east to west. The walls are almost vertical and
fold outwards or widen at water level to form cavities of rocky limestone. From
the mouth of the well to the water level there is a depth of 22 metres, and from
there to the bottom another 20 metres of water with muddy sediments in places
reaching four metres in depth, particularly in the centre. The greenish hue of the
waters is due to the presence of algae and micro-organisms, and also to the shadow
cast by the vegetation growing all around the *cenote (Fig.72)*.

The rocky mouth of the well, particularly on the south side, is slightly fa-
shioned to the extent of showing a kind of grading on two levels, perhaps to better
accomodate the public that would have participated in the ceremonies. On the
south side was a building with two rooms, one with an entrance facing east and
the other facing west. The building was modified later as the western room was
converted into a *temazcal,* or steam bath to purify the sacrificial victims. There
was also an irregular platform built on to the edge of the well, from where the sacrificial victims may have been hurled down to the bottom of the well. Tooled
stones similar to those seen on the panels in the Ball Court can be seen on this

72. The Cenote of Sacred Well.

platform. The repeated usage of these, indicates that the practice of sacrifice in the
Cenote was a late one, even though earlier the Itzá would have carried out offerings
to the god of the water.

Roads

A vital element in the Itzá city was the construction of roads or *sacbés*. These enabled the population to move freely and gave them access to the different groups of
religious and administrative buildings, linking these with existing districts or sub-
centres. In Chichén there are at least eight roads or internal causeways built from
compressed stone and *sascab*. They all appear to start out from the main square of
the Castle or Main temple of Kukulcán and cover altogether some three kilomet-
res.

One road or causeway goes from the Castle to the Sacred Cenote (170 metres
long). Another leaves from the Ball Court leading westwaards for 700 metres. Another sets off from the Castle towards the Nunnery for 300 metres and from there a
different road continues towards the Group of the Three Lintels for 1000 metres.
One more goes from the Observatory or Caracol to the Cenote Xtoloc and is 200
metres long, whilst another goes eastwards from the Thousand Columns for 150
metres. Finally, there is a causeway, 220 metres long, that leaves Hacienda Chichén and goes towards the group of the Hieroglyphic Jambs. All these complete a
true road network *(General plan).*

The Final Events

As we have already seen, the city of Mayapán was conquered by the people who resided on the outside of the city walls. Chichén Itzá and Uxmal were abandoned and
with this commenced the disintegration of the major lordships (señoríos) that had
controlled the large region of Yucatán.

The "Books of Chronicles" of *Chilam Balam de Chumayel* writes:

> 1 Ahau [1382-1401]. This was when the remainder of the Itzá were driven out of
> Chichén.
> It was the third tun of Katun 1 Ahau when Chichén was depopulated
> [destroyed]. It was in the first tun of Katun 1 Ahau that the head chief Tutul Xiu

departed with the chiefs of the town and the four divisions of the town [cantzuculcab]. This was the katun when the men of Tancah were dispersed and the chiefs of the town were scattered.

8 Ahau [1441-1461]. This was the katun when the remainder of the Itzá founded their town coming forth from beneath the trees and bushes at Tan-Xuluc-Mul, as it was called. They came out and established the land of Zaclactun Mayapán ... In the seventh tun of Katun 8 Ahau, this was the katun when Chakánputún perished at the hands of Kak-u-pacal and Tec Uilu.

8 Ahau was the katun when occurred the arrival of the remainder of the Itzá as they were called. They arrived, and their reign endured in Chakánputún. 8 Ahau was when their town was abandoned and they were scattered throughout the entire district.

In the sixth Ahau [1461-1480] after they were dispersed, then they ceased to be called Maya.

11 Ahau [1539-1559] was the name of the Katun when the Maya men ceased to be called Maya. They were called Christians; their entire province <became subject> to St. Peter and the reigning king of <Spain>.

11 Ahau was when the mighty men [men of God] arrived from the East. They were the ones who first brought <disease> here to our land, <the land of> us who are Maya, in the year 1513.

11 Ahau, that was the Katun, when the Spaniards first arrived here in our land. It was in the seventh tun of Katun 11 Ahau that Christianity then began, it was in the year A. D. 1519.

Thus, around the year 1400 A. D. Chichén Itzá was depopulated. Also at this time Uxmal was abandoned by the Xiu who went to Maní, whilst some of the Itzá went on to Champotón. These Itzá or possibly others, reached as far as Tayasal in the Itzá Petén. With such separations, the Maya ceased to call themselves Maya, and on the arrival of the Spaniards and Christianity the people of Yucatán were converted into Maya-Christians. The dates when the Spaniards entered the Peninsular were known precisely and amongst the dates recorded are the arrival and stay amongst the Maya of Aguila y Guerrero (1513), the discovery of Hernández de Córdoba (1517), of Cortés (1519), the foundation of Campeche and the expedition of Montejo to Calkiní and Yucatán (1540 and 1541). The foundation of Mérida (1542) is also recorded. The conquest of the Itzá who had sought refuge in the Petén took place in 1697.

There were no longer good priests to educate us. That is the origin of the Seat of the second time, the reign of the second time. It is also the cause of our death. We no longer had good priests, we no longer had knowledge, and in the end worth and shame were lost. And all were equal.

Summary

The history of Chichén Itzá can be summarised in the following way. In approximately 415-435 A. D. a group of Mayas from the south of the Peninsula discovered and occupied Bacalar, Quintana Roo. From there, some members of this group discovered and occupied Chichén (at that time the site did not have this name). They began the construction of the first buildings displaying a combination of architectural styles of the Chen and Puuc (495- 514). Two hundred years later, some of the inhabitants of Chichén inexplicably abandoned the city and went to Champotón, Campeche (672-692). These people arrived and settled in Champotón in 692-711. Meanwhile, the remainder of the population of Chichén continued to develop the culture there, and to construct buildings.

The Itzá tribe, who were Maya-Chontal in origin, extended from Tabasco to the Laguna de Términos, Campeche. They emigrated along the Gulf Coast and reached Champotón in 711-731. There, they settled and remained for approximately two hundred years until 928-948. They then left and moved westwards towards Yucatán, accompanied by other tribes. In 968-987 they arrived in Chichén (which indeed now was called Chichén Itzá), meaning "Mouth of the well of the wise man of the water".

The Itzá introduced the cult of Kukulcán, accompanying it with the practice of militarism. The cult imposed a series of new cultural elements amongst which are yokes, "palmas", the phallic cult, clay nose adornments, and depictions of streams of blood gushing from the throat of a decapitated serpent on the sculptures. These elements have different origins. The cult to Quetzalcóatl or Venus as the man-bird-serpent, as creator of the Fifth Sun and of the new humanity, as lord of time or of the year, originates in Xochicalco, Morelos. Architectural elements from this area include the beautiful plumed serpents, sloping and vertical walls on the buildings and jambs decorated in bas-relief. The leafy scrolls, belts with centres finished off in serpents, arm protectors in the form of round disks and sandals with knots in the form of serpents are characteristic of the pacific Coast of Guatemala and the Usumacinta region. All these elements are mixed with the traditional Chen-Puuc styles from Chichén and they combine to form a style called Maya-Yucatec. It has been incorrectly supposed that this style was of Toltec origin, from Tula, Hidalgo.

The Itzá governed Chichén by means of High priests who had the same name as the deity (for example, Kukulcanes (Mizcit Ahau, perhaps Kukulcán I; Ah Nacxit Kukulcán or Ah Kukulcán, Kukulcán II; Chac Xib Chac). The Itzá forged an alliance with Uxmal and Mayapán, with the Xiu and Cocom who followed the cult of Kukulcán (Hapai Can), as also did the people of Izamal. During this time (987-1185) they built buildings with the characteristic cultural elements already mentioned (those stongly linked to the religion and cult to Quetzalcóatl or Kukulcán).

Due to the ambition of Hunac Ceel Cauich of Mayapán the alliance with Uxmal and Mayapán broke. With troops and Mexican (nahuat) captains Hunac Ceel attacked and conquered Chichén around 1185-1204. As a result. the governor of Chichén, Chac- Xib-Chac, with his men and those of Uxmal, abandoned the site, thus starting a migration or exodus to several parts of Yucatán, leaving from the east. Hunac Ceel enthroned himself in Chichén and followed the cult to the Sun and to War, the cult of Ah Mex Cuc. This deity appears to be a version of Kukulcán, as a bearded man and related to the sun, fire and war. These aspects of the cult can be seen reflected in other buildings in Chichén.

After the hegemony of Mayapán (1204-1441), and after several uprisings, the city was destroyed in 1441-1461. With the destruction of Mayapán Chichén Itzá also collapsesd, already by this time largely depopulated, although archeological discoveries show that the site continued inhabited in part and continued to be a site of pilgramage.

Some of the buildings that we contemplate today were built between 1185 and 1401, in the Maya-Yucatec style of the earlier period. Now, however, certain new elements that are related more with war and with the sun are added. It is these elements in particular that are to be seen in Tula, Hidalgo, due to the influence of Chichén over this site during the time of Quetzalcóatl (II) who was a contemporary of Huemac, the last governor of Tula.

The architectural styles can be divided in different periods. A first period dated from 500 A. D. to 950 A. D. is observed in Chichén characterised by the Chen and Puuc styles. Here, the notable buildings are set on low platforms, the facade panels are plain, there are plain plinths between mouldings, several chambers with multiple rooms, vaulted roofs made from cut stone, lintels and jambs of plain stone, sometimes hieroglyphic inscriptions on the lintels, plain friezes between plain cornice mouldings, crests on the fronts of the buildings, masks of Chac and fret patterns in stone mosaic decorating the crests. All is carried out with an eye to symmetry.

During the evolution of the Puuc style, other elements are assimilated such as the decorated friezes, decorated cornice mouldings, buildings of few rooms, sometimes with rounded corners, simple stairways, central roof crests, totally decorated facades (Chen style) and other decorative elements. Amongst these, for example, are masks of Chac, chevron decorations simulating a band broken with inverted triangles, fret patterns, panels of cross-hactching, fluted columns and half columns on the corners as part of the decoration. All of these elements can be found amongst the buildings at Chichén ranging in complexity from the Akab Dzib to the Nunnery, passing through The Church, the Temple of the Three Lintels, the Chinchanchob, the House of the Deer and the Annex to the Nunnery, in quantative order according to the number of quoted elements (Diagram 1).

The arrival of the Itzá and the foreign influences that accompanied the cult of Kukulcán or Quetzalcóatl made an impact in the Puuc culture, initiating the new architectural style called Maya-Yucatec. The local builders and sculptors adapted their style to the newly introduced ideas. We see clearly, how particular elements of the Puuc tradition such as a sense of symmetry, stone mosaic, vaulted roofs, masks of Chac, plain facade panels, plain or decorated cornice mouldings, sculptures in relief, bases, buildings on platforms and decorated friezes were combined with other aspects that gradually appeared on the site. Amongst the new elements are the decorated ball courts, circular based buildings, bas-relief panels, realistic plumed serpents, intertwined serpents, sloping and vertical walls, balustraded staircases and decorated balustrades.

Exemplary buildings include the Ball Court and the Caracol. Other artisitic elements are the representations of decaptitated ball game players, blood in the form of serpents, scrolls and leafy volutes, yoke-belts, "palmas", rounded disks, back disks, pectorals in the form of cut conch shells, clay nose adornments and many others.

At a specific moment columns decorated in bas-relief appear, as also decorated jambs, decorated vaulting, panels with representations of the man-bird-serpent or Kukulcán, jaguar thrones, serpents forming an S shape, pectorals in the form of butterflies and the practice of the phallic cult. At the same time, square pillars decorated with warriors, vestibules with porticos, little drums from the Puuc style, serpentine columns, painted murals, wooden lintels, walking jaguars, war shields, chacmools, serpentine pillars, plain, raised panels giving the idea of capes (or scapularies) and representations of priests and lords are introduced. Buildings displaying these aspects include the North Temple or Temple of the Beareded Man, the South Temple and the Temple of the Tigers, all of which are built within the Ball Court, and constructed a few years later than that building. Other structures featuring these elements are the Annex to the Tigers and Substructures of the Warriors and the Castle.

As a consequence of the conquest of Chichén Itzá, the raised panels and sunken spaces appear with representations of eagles and jaguars eating human hearts. Numerous other aspects are notable at this time, in particular standard bearers, painted murals with battle scenes, mausoleums or bases with four steps, *tzompantli* or skull altars, castellations on the roofs of the buildings, decorated benches, colonnades and Atlantes and Caryatids. Others include rooms with columns and capitals, decorations on the sloping walls and also on the panels, cube shaped blocks with projecting serpents heads, serpents heads at the feet of the balustrades and representations of Tlalchitonatiuh. These elements are visible on the buildings known as Temple of the Warriors, The Castle, Temple of the Eagles and Tigers, Annex to the Caracol, the Tzompantli, Temple of the Atlantes and others (Diagram 1).

The first period of the Maya-Yucatec style dates from 950-1000 to 1150-1200 A. D. marks the gradual unfolding of Chichén Itzá. A second period from 1150-1200 to 1350-1400, under the influence of Mayapán, received late Mexican influences from the mercenary soldiers and captains who perhaps came from Xicalango, Campeche.

In both periods, however, there is a marked unity of style, as ancient elements are continued without displacing the native Puuc-Chen traditions of the site. There is no doubt that the Maya-Yucatec style originated and extended to several parts of the Yucatán Peninsular (Uxmal, Mayapán, Tulum, Cozumel, San Miguel, Chunyaxché) and even exerted influence on Tula, Hidalgo, especially towards the end of the first period and beginning of the second.

SOCIETY AND CULTURE

73. Stela number 3 from Xochicalco, Morelos. Shows a Quetzalcóatl as Lord of the Year or of cyclical time.

ANTECEDENTS

At the end of the "Peoples and Theocratic States" period in Mesoamerica, at the time of the disintegration of the large cities and religious centres, several tribal groups moved frequently from place to place, wandering in search of new lands on which to settle. They emigrated to sites promised by their principal gods or patrons, before forming themselves into townships and establishing their lineages. On this basis, it is possible to explain certain concepts that appear in the historical sources, amongst which we can mention the following problematical expressions: "see the light", "new dawn and new lord" and "go together under the guidance of the four caudillos, four chiefs, four carriers of god or four groups of people, and suffer penances before reaching the promised land".

Before the Mexicas, the migratory pattern was common amongst other groups, such as the Toltecs, Teotenacas, Itzá, Xiu, Quiché and others in the Mesoamerican area, whose migrations constitute the historical basis with which to justify their existence or, their *raison d'etre*. It is this very same history which, from a different point of view, contains elements taken from myths and legends, linking origins to a god and high priests who used the same name as the deity.

Amongst these migratory groups, the deity was Quetzalcóatl, born in Xochicalco, Morelos and whose cult extended as far as the Maya lands. His name was translated in the different regional dialects and languages by means of the high priests or chiefs who used the same name. Quetzalcóatl (man-bird-serpent) was also called Kukulcán, Gucumatz, Tohil, Kukulchán, Nacxitl, Votán, Mizcit, Xuchit, Cezalcuati, the same as the high priests.

Representations of lifelike, plumed serpents symbolizing Quetzalcóatl are to be found in Xochicalco, Morelos. The human face also appears coming out of the fangs of the beautiful, plumed serpent (man-bird-serpent). Quetzalcóatl is also represented as a Tláloc, with eyeglasses, moustache, fangs and with carvings of the year hieroglyph (intertwined triangles and rectangles), which can be identified with the rain, agriculture, vegetation, the year and the time cycle *(Fig.73)*.

This representation of Quetzalcóatl or Venus as lord of Time is the best indication of the propagation of his cult into the Maya lands. It permits the dating of his creation and the dispersal of certain groups, and the high priests who, accompanied

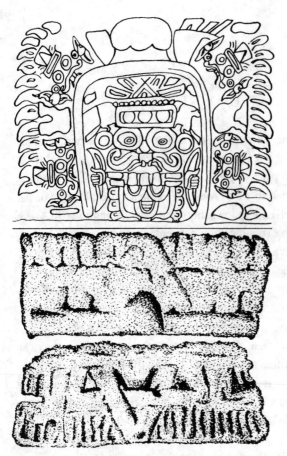

74. Sculptures from the Pacific Coast of Guatamala, which illustrate the cult to the Lord of the Year, or Quetzalcoatl.

by militarism carried the religion to distant lands. On the coasts of Guatamala we can see sculptures of flat stones with bas-reliefs representing Quetzalcóatl as lord of Time demonstrated either by the engraving of a year hieroglyph (triangle-rectangle) or by the depiction of a face of Tláloc with a year marking occupying a central position, surrounded by four small Tlálocs, with the same markings facing the cardinal points *(Fig. 74)*.

In Guatamala, principally on the Pacific Coast, there is an associated artistic style, which is reflected on great natural rocks formations or on formal sculptures. These show the predominance of representations of humans or gods with their hair in the form of lifelike, plumed serpents, belts finished off with decorations of tails and heads of serpents, sandals with knotted serpents and knee plates or disks in the form of serpents. A further important feature of that style is the custom of filling the empty spaces in the principal scenes with elaborate festoons, of foliage, flow-

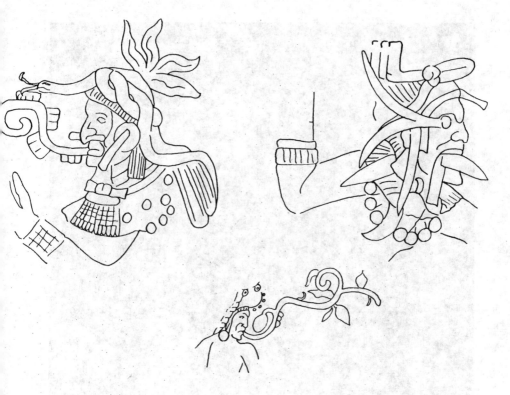

75. Drawings of dignatories found on Monument 21 in Bilbao, Guatemala.

ers, animals and fruits. Sometimes, the figures have floral volutes or a leafy garland coming out of their mouths *(Figs 75, 76)*.

Clearly, there are other characteristics in those sculptures which are also worth pointing out. Amongst these are the depiction of the god with flames, symbolizing fire or the Sun, the wearing of yokes on the belts and the use of knee adornments. Other practices recorded on the sculptures are the offering of decapitated heads relating to the Ball Court, staffs with one end curved and representations of temples. These are characteristics which reveal Gulf Coast (of Mexico) influences and which were fused together to create that new style which then passed on to the High lands of Guatemala, from there to spread to the Usumacinta region and the low lands *(Fig. 77)*.

This style from the Pacific Coast of Guatemala (Bilbao, El Baúl, Escuintla), with influences from the Mexican Gulf Coast and Xochicalco, penetrated into the

76. Monument number 21 from Bilbao, Guatemala.

low lands, in some cases superimposing itself over the classic Maya style or fusing with it. In Stela 2 at Aguateca in the Guatemalen Petén there is a noble warrior carrying a lance and a rectangular shield, decorated with the effigy of the sun god. He is clearly identifyable because of the bulging and projecting eyes. The figure wears a skirt and an apron which shows the face of Tláloc, or Lord of Time (one aspect of Quetzalcoátl). He wears a kind of shirt and over this a collar-cape covered with beads or chalchihuites. From his neck hangs a bird shaped pectoral (*totol* or bird). There are also hanging knee adornments and his feet are like the talons of a bird of prey. On the headdress of splendid feathers one can observe the year hieroglyph (triangle-rectangle). This stela has an inscription —9.15.0.0.0 or 9.16.0.0.0— corresponding to the years 711-751 A. D. *(Fig. 78)*.

In Seibal, Guatemala, there are several stelas that show the penetration of a

77. Monument number 6
from Bilbao, Guatemala.

people somewhat different to the Maya of that site, relating to the theme under discussion. On Stela 13 we see a lord dressed in a frontal-bandage, from whose edges hang serpents. The bandage in turn is supported by a band or belt in the form of a plaited serpent. He wears a horizontal, clay nose adornment, a circular ear decoration and bracelets. Viewed from the back we see his long hair and a face resembling the sun god. Coming out of his mouth is a large, floral volute symbolizing the Word or Song *(Fig. 79).*

On another Seibal Stela we see a richly decorated Lord where amongst the most notable elements are the ear pieces, the maniqui-sceptre finished with the head of a serpent and the figure of the god of the rain or perhaps, Itzam-ná. Also, on the edge of the bandage are engravings of twisted stone seats symbolizing Pop, representing lordship or power and perhaps Venus. On Stela 10 is a figure with ear pieces and clay nose adornment, decorated with masks of the heavenly sun god (Itzam-ná), who also has a moustache and a cotton collar-cape decorated with *chal-*

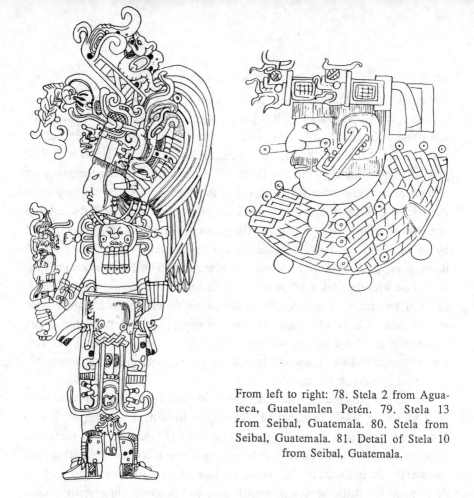

From left to right: 78. Stela 2 from Aguateca, Guatelamlen Petén. 79. Stela 13 from Seibal, Guatemala. 80. Stela from Seibal, Guatemala. 81. Detail of Stela 10 from Seibal, Guatemala.

chihuites or beads and twisted stone engravings or Pop hieroglyphs. This stela is dated around 849 A. D., but in Seibal there are others which go back to 750 A. D., and as a consecuence it is possible to date the foreign intrusion from 750-850 A. D. *(Figs. 80, 81).*

In accordance with Thompson (1970), the penetration by foreigners can also be seen in Altar de Sacrificios, Guatemala, where Stela 15 can be dated to between 751-771 A. D. (9.17.0.0.0) and in Ucamal on a stela dating to 849 A. D. In Yaxchilán, Chiapas, Lintel 25 shows a beautiful serpent from whose jaws emerges a humanised god, and we can also mention Bonampak, Chiapas, where Stela 2 shows a richly decorated priest with a bag of *copal,* accompanied by two women. One of the women has a decoration of the two faces of the Lord of Time in the form of Tláloc on the lower edge of her *huipil* (native dress), accompanied by three year hieroglyphs.

It is, therefore, possible to conclude the following. The artistic customs of

Mexican Gulf Coast influenced the Pacific Coast of Guatemala introducing yokes, "palmas", axes, decapitation of ball game players, clay nose adornments, scrolls and volutes. Xochicalco, Morelos, contributed to the diffusion of the new culture with the introduction of the cult to Quetzalcóatl depicted as a Tláloc with year glyph and as the Lord of Time. On the Pacific Coast of Guatemala an artistic style formed that was characterized by the cult to the serpent. This style can be seen in the hair, belts, knots of the sandals and knee decorations, and also in the festoons or intertwined foliage patterns that fill the spaces between the scenes, accompanied by animals, fruits and flowers. There are also representations of the solar god. All these characteristics passed on to the low lands of the Petén and the Usumacinta and mixed with the Classic Maya traditions in Seibal, Aguateca, Altar de Sacrificios and Yaxchilán. From this mixture of cultures the concept of Itzam-ná (wise man of the clouds, he who makes the rain) originated. In turn, the people of this region dispersed towards Nonoualco-Zuyúa (Tabasco-Laguna de Términos) from where the Xiu and the Itzá would later leave for Yucatán. In general terms, this was to occur between 700 and 900 A. D.

We have already seen that the Xiu came from from Tulapan Chiconoauhtlan on the Gulf Coast, which is perhaps El Tajín (city towards the Nautla). It is also known that the Xiu were in Nonoualco (Tabasco) and that later they moved to Chacnabitón and Uxmal, there introducing the cult to Kukulcán or Quetzalcóatl. Meanwhile, the Itzá were in Chakanputún (Champotón) or lands of Zuyúa (Laguna de Términos), and also headed westwards towards Yucatán, settling finally in Chichén Itzá.

However, according to the *Chilam Balam de Chumayel,* four groups set off from the site denominated as Nine Mountains. One group came from Kincolah Petén, one from Nacocob, another group came from Five Mountains and the other from Holtún Zuyúa. Thus, groups of peoples including the Xiu and the Itzá, came from a southerly region, mountainous and with low lands, corresponding to the territory now known as the Petén in Chiapas-Guatemala. Other groups came from the Gulf Coast displaying a culture that reflected a mixture of characteristics originating on the Pacific Coast of Guatemala, from the Peten and the Usumacinta, from the Gulf Coast of Mexico and from Xochicalco in Central High Plateau, as has already been shown.

Thus, the Xiu settled in lands close to Uxmal, where, according to the Chumayel, "the priests reveered Chac, the priests of the ancient times; and it was then that Hapai Can was brought to Chemchan; when he arrived they marked the walls of Uxmal with blood)". The Xiu group brought the cult of the serpent or Ku-kulcán with them arriving at a place called Chemchan, neighbouring Uxmal, which we are now able to identify as Mul Chic, located between Santa Elena Nac-ocob and Uxmal.

Mul Chic or Chemchan was a small ceremonial centre during the Classic Maya period. It had a few buildings distributed around the square. In particular these were single roomed structures built on low platforms or plinths, with crudely vaulted roofs and roof combs on the wall facades. In one of the rooms the remains of a painted mural which would once have covered all four walls has been found showing the conquest of the site by a foreign group.

In this painting, one observes a battle scene in which individuals appear, fighting with stones, knives, and ropes. A processional scene follows showing high priests wearing large headdresses and masks and with serpents coming out of their mouths. They also are decorated with clay nose adornments and belts decorated with serpents, carry shields, and wear protective, puffed sleeves on their arms. There is another scene of warriors, sometimes covered in black, carrying shields, *macanas* (like machetes or scythes) with flint or obsidian edges and wearing strips of leather or cloth finishing in serpents and earpieces. A further scene shows sacrificial priests covered in black with knives or daggers in their hands, skulls hanging from their chests and lords with their hands tied behind their backs, ready to be sacrificed. The figure of the conquering lord, now very much damaged, can also be seen. He is dressed in a skirt and at his head level is the blue bird which is the symbol of his name (Tutul Xiu) *(Fig. 84)*.

From these paintings it is possible to see that the people under the command of the Xiu used many of the traits that have already been described in relation to Quetzalcóatl, such as clay nose adornments, ear pieces, belts finished with serpents, sceptres or staffs with curved ends, shields and collars inlaid with chalchi-huites. Other elements, however, also appear, such as strips that are crossed over or rolled and knotted and finished in serpents, a series of circular rings on the arms, serpents coming out of the mouths, masks resembling Chac and Itzam-ná, wooden *macanas* with one end curved and with incrusted edges, decapitated heads, black painted bodies and faces, crossed tibias and tall, feathered headdresses. All of these are traits that can been seen in Uxmal and Chichén Itzá *(Fig. 83)*.

From historical sources we know that the Xiu conquered Uxmal, dominated the original population, related to the Puuc or Serranía, and introduced their customs, religion and artistic ideas that were then assimilated by the Maya of the area. We

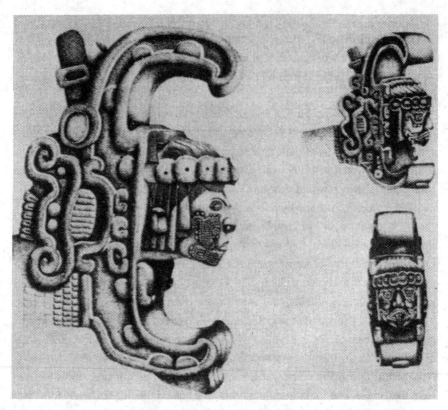

82. Sculptures representing Kukulcán. From The Magician, at Uxmal, Yucatán.

can see how the sculptures of Kukulcán appeared, beautifully tooled, showing the god coming out of the jaws of the serpent, with the cheek incised and a turban of beads or chalchihuites, sometimes with solar eyes and with the tail of the rattlesnake coming out of his mouth *(Fig. 82)*.

These sculptures —that have a spike to fix them in place— decorate the first building known as the Temple of the Magician. This structure should date from the times of the Xiu conquest. The building was also decorated with mouldings with a series of rings or bells (like the tail of the rattlesnake), rectangles with intertwining foliage and a god with eye-rings and crossed tibias. There are panels with effigies of the Lord of Time, in the style of Tláloc with eye-rings, moustache, fangs, open mouth and three, year glyphs (triangle and recatangle intertwined) on the front and with ears very similar to those from Xochicalco, Morelos.

Of course, there is further evidence of the Xiu occupation in Uxmal. In the North Building of the Nunnery are masks of the Lord of Time with the tongue in

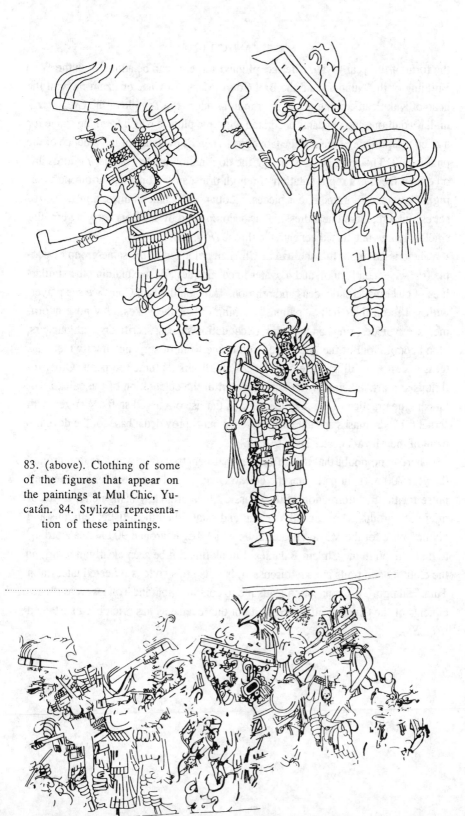

83. (above). Clothing of some of the figures that appear on the paintings at Mul Chic, Yucatán. 84. Stylized representation of these paintings.

the form of the year glyph. Lifelike, plumed serpents can be admired on the West Building of the Nunnery and the Ball Court. Masks of Chac or Itzam-ná with the head of Kukulcán coming out of their mouths adorn the Temple of the Great Pyramid. Medallions and pendants decorated with fine plumes which form the frame for a fixed sculpture are seen on The Governor. There is evidence of the practice of the phallic cult. There are stelas showing the domination of the conquering lords and on one of these is a representation of a high priest sitting on a jaguar throne wearing a clay nose adornment, ear pieces, a collar with chalchihuites, arm rings, rosettes and a feathered headdress. He is accompanied by warriors carrying circular shields, lying vanquished beneath the throne *(Fig. 85)*.

There is no doubt that the Itzá of Chichén belonged to the same group of people (*its,* wise man [brujo], and *a,* water in cakchiquel), thus explaining the similarities of customs, artistic ideas and religion. Thus, on the Ball Court we see players with yokes on their belts, "palmas" coming out of the yokes, clay nose adornments, ear pieces, rings on the arms, decapitation scenes, sacrificers with daggers, blood coming out of the throats stylized in the form of serpents, intertwined patterns or festoons filling the empty spaces and lifelike, plumed serpents. Other religious and artistic similarities can be noted in the celebration of the cult to Kukulcán, the practice of the phallic cult, and the use of curved staffs, sceptres with serpents heads, masks and shields. These elements provided a base for the development of the Maya-Yucatec style *(Fig. 87)*.

There is no doubt that the influences that penetrated the Maya region around the year 700 A. D., in particular the cult to Quetzalcóatl, were the formulative impulse for the transformation of the Classic Maya art. They instigated a series of migratory groups who reached Yucatán and established the artistic, religious and cultural base for the Maya-Yucatec style which began around 900 A. D. according to dates given in the Chilam Balames. I think this can be seen clearly, not only in the clothing and traits already discussed, but also this style is reflected later on in Tula, Hidalgo. This connection leads me to conclude that the Toltecs were the recipients of the Chichén influence, and not the reverse as has often been sustained *(Fig. 86)*.

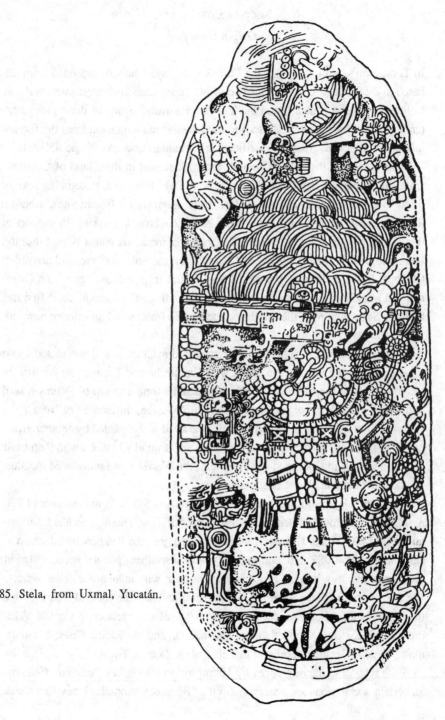

85. Stela, from Uxmal, Yucatán.

Origin of the Itzá

In Thompson's opinion (1970), the Putuns and Maya-Chontals extended from Tabasco to the Grijalva-Usumacinta. They were expert seabourne merchants, and controlled the trading routes round the Yucatán Penisular. Some of these groups extended from Champotón (Tabasco) to the Usumacinta which explains the foreign influences in Seibal, Altar de Sacrificios and Ucanal, between 750 and 850 A. D.

One branch of the Maya-Chontal, the Itzá, settled in the island of Cozumel, from where they crossed the sea and arrived in Polé, from there penetrating into the interior of the Yucatán Penisula. Here, they conquered different sites, amongst them Chichén Itzá around the year 918 A. D. (2 Akbal, 1 Yaxkín). In support of this migration, the *Chilam Balam de Chumayel* mentions that it is said that the Itzá multiplied in the litle island of Cuzamil, left for Polé, Aké etc. and arrived at Chichén. It also mentions that the Maya-Chontal from Acalan came from Cozumel and founded their capital in Izancanac. According to Thompson, these first Itzá built the Substructure of the Castle, painted battle frescos and introduced new cultural elements.

This researcher also states that the Itzá settled in Chichén and dominated a vast region, conserving links in the South with Campeche and Tabasco, so facilitating the migration to the west by another group. This time a group of Putuns mixed with Nahaut speakers, or rather, a group with Mexican influences or from Tula, Hidalgo. Thompson suggests that Kukulcán arrived accompanied by another group of Putún-Itzá with greater influence, from Tula, around 970 A. D., who then built the Castle, the Ball Court and the Temple of the Warriors and introduced metalurgy and other cultural characteristics.

Thus, for Thompson one group of Itzá arrived in 918 A. D. and another in 970 A. D., the latter group influenced by the Toltecs of Tula, Hidalgo, as has been sustained for many years. However, we affirm here, that the Itzá penetrated into Yucatán around 968-987 A. D. and that they were a southern people, because *itzá* in cakchiquel means wise man of the water (from *its*, wise man, and *a* or *ha*, water). We also affirm that they were in Chontal lands and that the cultural elements that they introduced, amongst them the cult to Kukulcán, are related to Central Veracruz, The Huasteca, Xochicalco, the Usumacinta and the Pacific Coast of Guatemala. These styles are not present in Tula and predate the Toltecs.

With respect to the references by Thompson to the *Chilam Balam de Chumayel,* certain acclarations are necessary. In the "Book of Chronicles" they first speak

86. (above). Clothing of the Itzá: a) Teotihuacan-Tikal. b) Mul Chic, Yucatán. c) Chichén Itzá, Ball Court. d, e) Chichén Itzá, Annex of the Tigers. f) Chichén Itzá, pillars from the Warriors. g) Ixtapantongo, México. h,i,j) Tula, Hidalgo.

of the organization of the land: of the four directions of the world with their four colours, four trees, four gods and four stones. Then, it speaks of the chiefs who settled in the four parts of the land. Continuing, the *Chilam Balam* says: "Then they swarmed at Cozumel in great numbers among the magueys" without specifically mentioning the Itzá. After referring to Mayapán and Hunac Ceel, who was ambitious for power, the *Chilam Balam* continues "Whereupon they departed and arrived at Ppoole...Then They arrived at Aké...". There is no specific mention that

87. Detail of the players from the reliefs on the Ball Court at Chichén Itzá.

they left from Cozumel, Thompson's personal interpretation.

In fact, the + recounts the formation of the world or of the land starting with the gods. Christian concepts are intermingled with the prehispanic culture recalling the *Popul Vuh,* or sacred book of the Quiché. Paraphrasing the *Chumayel* we find the following description of the creation or formation of the world. Ah Mucen Cab (the keeper of the honey) sold his eyes to the Thirteen Gods (of the heavens) and the Thirteen Gods were caught by the Nine Gods (of the darkness) and it rained fire and ashes. They took the white beans and ground them up together with their semen; and with their heart they ground the fine seed of the marrow or gourd and also the large seeds, together with ground black beans. He, who is eternal, mixed it all together, and bound it together and went to the thirteenth ring of the heavens. And when the Great Serpent was stolen, the firmament collapsed and sunk the Earth. Then the Four Bocab levelled everything out. And the First White Tree grew up in the north; the First Black Tree, in the west; the First Yellow Tree in the south; and the Great Mother Ceiba grew up. And Chac Piltec (god of the east) rose up, then Zac Piltec (god of the north), Lahun Chan (of the west) and Kan Piltec (of the south).

But it was over the whole world that Ah Uuc Cheknal was set up. He came from the seventh stratum of the earth, when he came to fecundate Itzam-kab-ain. They

moved among the four lights, among the four layers of the stars. The world was
not lighted; there was neither day nor night nor moon. Then they perceived that
the world was being created. Then creation dawned upon the world...

When the world was submerged, when there was neither heaven nor earth, the
three cornered precious stone of grace was born, after the divinity of the ruler
was created, when there was no heaven. Then there wer born seven tuns, seven
katuns, hanging in the heart of the wind, the seven chosen ones...

<These are> the angels of the winds which were set up while he created the
star, when the world was not yet lighted, when there was neither heaven nor
earth: the Red Pauahtun, the White Pauahtun, the Black Pauahtun, the Yellow
Pauahtun...

4 Ahau [948-987] was the name of the katun when occurred the birth of the
Pauahs, when the rulers descended...

4 Ahau was the katun when they sought and discovered Chichén Itzá...They
became lords when they descended upon Chichén Itzá. The Itzá were they then
called.

Then several others arrived. Ah Ppisté, measurer of the lands; Chacté Abán, the
preparer and cultivator of the lands; Uac Habnal, the marker of the boundaries; and
Ah Ppisul, the measurer of the width and length of the lands.

Next, chiefs were established for each of the areas east, north, west and south.
The Great Bees were established on the cardinal points, red, white, black and yellow. The sons of the Bees (of the men) multiplied. The land was measured and
lands were founded for them and these lands were irrigated. It was then that it
dawned for them, New Lord, new awakening of earth for them, for the Itzá who
were created out of darkness, who were created by Mizcit Ahau.

Economic context

At the time the Itzá occupied the region and basing our knowledge on references in
the *Chumayel*, it is likely that in a lowland area the Itzá would have known plants
and trees such as: Ceiba, *pochote, chakán, pich,* incense tree *(copal),* indigo, *jabín,*
mahogany, *chacté, cocoyol,* sapodilla (gum tree), annona, mammee, *balché,* guano
palm, and perhaps also *nancen,* avocado, pawpaw and guayava. They also had
knowledge of maize, beans, marrow, chillie, *chaya, macal,* yam, *jícama cimarrona,*
guaje, henequén, cocoa, *ramón,* cotton and perhaps tobacco.

The different animals of the region were the following: deer, wild boar *(Kekén),* armadillo *(huech)*, wild turkey *(guajolote, cutz)*, pheasant, tapir, quail *(bech'ob)*, partridge, grouse, jaguar *(balam)*, iguana *(uo)*, bees and many others. There were also *cenotes* for drinking water, stone and lime quarries, flint, fire wood, tall and slim tree trunks and other primary materials.

From the region's flora one could gather wood for construction of the local huts in a variety of forms, such as cross bars, poles, gravel *(morillos)*, beams, climbing plants, lianas and guano palm). The plants also provided fibres for weaving such as cotton, *henequén* (sisal), hemp, *(pochote)*. They extracted dyes (indigo) and incense *(copal)*. The bark served for making paper *(amate)* and for the preparation of *balché* (drink made from certain fermented roots used in ceremonies). The wood was used for making lintels, particularly from the *chicozapote* or gum tree. They picked the wild fruits, most commonly annona, mamme or *cocoyol* and harvested cultivated plants (maize, beans, chillie, marrow or gourds, *chayote* etc.) and gathered plants such as *ramón, chaya, macal, jícama* and *cimarrona*. Tabacco, cocoa, and perhaps other plants were controlled under cultivation. They also knew of other plants for medicinal and other uses. The rural or peasant *(campesino)* populations were self-sufficient, practising agriculture, hunting and gathering and by combining their freetime with certain manual labours and the exploitation of the raw materials that they had to hand.

With the arrival of the Itzá, Chichén was already a theocratic city of some importance, governed by high priests who exploited the village communities to extract a surplus of food and labour, a condition which worsened with the conquest of the site and its transformation into a military centre.

Naturally, the peasant communities —with their knowledge, tools, natural and human resources— obtained food, clothes, household goods and certain manufactured handcrafts, including also, some of their necessary tools. They cultivated different types (colours) of maize, several species of gourds, chillies and beans. They ate *macal* cooked in earth ovens, cassava, *chaya* leaves, deer, wild turkey, armadillo and other animals that they hunted. They collected wild fruits, wax and honey. They wove cotton for clothes and they knew how to make fire. They tooled bone, stone and wood for their furniture and new tools. They also ate tortillas, *atoles* (maize based porridge), *tamales* (maize dough bundles filled with pork, cooked in earth ovens), ground marrow seeds, young beans, corn on the cob cooked in earth ovens, and in times of famine, the fruit of the *ramón* tree.

These peasant communities, however, had to pay their tributes to the nearby ceremonial centres, and in particular to the chief-city where the government resided. The payment was both in the form of food and in labour and also included some prime raw materials and certain domestic handcraft products. A large proportion of village production was used in the maintenance of the city's ruling class, with the consequent impoverishment of the surrounding communities, whose members not only had to produce food and extract raw materials and products, but also had to give their labour for public works, for the cultivation of the nobles' lands, for service in the lords' houses, or as manservants to the soldiers in time of war. Thus, they constituted the exploited class that scarcely had the minimum necessary with which to live.

The existence of Chichén Itzá and its growth is explicable only by the work force and by the economic resources extracted from the peasant communities by the centralized government and the burocracy that governed in the head city of the province or region. The peasant communities remained dependent on the head city which in turn inverted the economic surplus in buildings, monuments, roads, squares and other public works in the city, as well as in the maintenance of the non-productive class who resided in the city.

Of course, outside the walls of the city were the nobles' lands, orchards and cocoa plantations cultivated by the peasants or servants. The tributes collected by the tax collectors were transferred to the city, in maize, beans, chillie, wild turkey (guajolote), deer or honey, including salt and cocoa which had to be acquired by the tributees to give to the city. They also collected woven goods such as cotton cloths and straw mats, as well as regional raw materials such as wax, incense (copal), resin, feathers, skins, dyes, wood, which were essential supplies for the city's artesans . These specialists produced certain manufactured goods which were then acquired by the village population on market day, or used in commercial interchanges by the professional traders.

The small or large villages exploited the resources of the region and were the labour force who rendered up part of what they obtained in food, prime raw materials and domestic products, whilst living in huts made of perishable substances in concentrated or disperse communities. Meanwhile, the head city was the political and religious centre which received and distributed the surplusses amongst the non-productive class, who in turn controlled the specialized artesans and the trade of the city, in a large and concentrated urban group with vast complexes of civil and religious buildings, with a multiplicity of functions.

The existence of several peasant villages dependent on the head city, the tribute system which the villagers yielded to the city, the artesan production, trade and the market that existed in the city, as well as the centralized religious and political power that the city exercised over the peasant communities, reveals that in the region dominated by Chichén Itzá an agricultural-artesanal and tribute-market mode of production prevailed. The means of production and the relations between producers were controlled by the centralized government, or the state apparatus.

The politcial and social aspect

The Itzá (wise men of the water) "arrived conquering by warfare" and settled at the mouth of the well (Chi-Chén). For this reason the principal structures are built around that great water deposit. The Itzá dominated the original population who had established their settlement in the south of the site. They began to redistribute lands amongst the chiefs and to receive tributes in goods and in labour, including the region of Zuyúa from where they had come. They occupied the site and organized the land, exercising their power and hegemony for many years.

As the conquering group, they monopolized the necessary knowledge for effective government, military organization and religious activities, placing it all under the control of the centralized government. The ancient leaders and important functionaries from the original Maya society were incorporated into the new society. The new city placed nobles, priests, magistrates, administrators, builders, traders and artisans in charge of political and public offices, religious and military posts, of justice and of law, of diplomacy, trade, handcrafts, astrology and other social and cultural aspects.

At the head of the government was the lord (señor) with a hereditary office, as descendant of the line of the tribal god. This god might originally have been called Mizcit Ahau or Kukulcán I, and may have introduced the religion and cult to this deity, as the first encarnation and first high priest of the Itzá. We now know that other governors were Ah Nacxitl Kukulcán or Ah Kukulcán (Kukulcán II) and also Chac Xib Chac (the red rain god of the east) in the period before Hunac Ceel of Mayapán conquered Chichén Itzá.

The ruling lord represented the divinity, the supreme judge, the chief of the army and perhaps also held responsability as priest. He had political, judicial, military and religious functions that entitled him to the titles Halach Uinic, Ahau, Ah Kin, Noh Yum Cab (great man, lord, priest of the Sun, great high pontifice). He was aided by the Batabes (those of the axe) or lesser chiefs of the suburbs and vil-

lages and also by the Balames (priests or seers). Other assistants were the Caluac
or tax collectors who collected the tributes, the Ah Kines or priests of the solar
cult, the Nacomes or sacrificers, and a whole range of individuals of different rank
and prestige in charge of the carrying out of community works, financial activities, military affairs, diplomatic affairs, commerce and general administration.

The upper class of Chichén Itzá was integrated by the lord, the nobles, the dis-
tinguished military, high ranking merchants, priests and some others, considered
to be the Almehenob, or the people of the lineage and those who carried out the
ruling offices, administrative, military and religious functions. These dignatories
were also traders and held some intelectual knowledge including astronomy,
knowledge of the calendar, numeracy, astrology, law, herbal medicine and others.

All these individual or ruling groups lived in the city and formed the state apparatus. By means of a physical and ideological coerction (military and religious)
these groups exercised power or dominion over the region and the village communities that fell into the city's orbit. The city was the seat of government, the home
of the upper classes, the centre of all political, economic and religious activities
and the expression of socioeconomic power. The privileged class controlled the
dues of the city and the artisan production, the distribution or use of the surplus,
the planning and organization of the tribute labour for the building of temples,
squares, roads, buildings and other public works, as much in the common interest
of the resident society as in their own or elitist interests.

There were also people in the city who carried out minor administrative or bu-
rocratic functions, other functionaries, small merchants, artisans and individuals
specialized in other activities (sculpters, weavers, painters, carpinters, engravers,
metalurgists, plumists, potters, cocoa planters) This group formed the middle class
or the Acmen Uinic, plebeyan men, or men of middle status or ranking.

A third and inferior class consisted of servants who worked the land for the
lords and for the State, or who worked as domestic servants in the temples, as
porters for the principal merchants, as soldiers in time of war, as labourers on the
public building sites or even as slaves obtained in the conquests who could be sold
or bartered and exchanged. The peasants, hunters and those dedicated to lesser tasks
in the villages are included in this social class.

At first, and to secure political stability in the conquered region, the Itzá
formed an alliance or union with the lords who governed other important neighbouring head cities, such as Uxmal, Mayapán and Izamal. These were also families
of lineage who had in common the religion of Kukulcán, the tribal god. This alli-

ance, (known as the League of Mayapán) permitted control over a greater population and a larger region (from where the soldiers were recruited for the wars of expansion and for the defense of their territory) and also allowed for the subjugation, tributing and protection of a number of small towns and villages. The League facilitated exchanges and trade and the redistribution of material goods within the territory. It also represented a ruling state or national entity, with both religious and civil power incarnated in the divinity Kukulcán.

Thus, within the territory or the State Federation, several ethnic groups or ruling houses (Cocoms, Itzá, Xiu, Itzamaleños) dominated a multitude of villages, resting points and rural areas. The head cities each had their own state government, controlled by community relations based on land ownership, on specialized labour, on the tributary and military obligations, and also in the religious cult and in trade supported by the work of full time artisans. Some of the city states were stronger than others, some having territorial differences reflected in both size and in availability of raw materials, which led to ambition for power supported by militarism. This was the case in Mayapán, leading to the destruction of the alliance and the launching of the offensive on Chichén Itzá.

Hunac Ceel Cauich of Mayapán vanquished Chichén Itzá using Mexican capitains. He expelled the lord Chac Xib Chac and occupied the seat or throne of the site, after passing the test of throwing himself into the *cenote,* or sacred well. Mayapán of the Cocom, with its mercenary soldiers, gained hegemony and socioeconomic power over the territory until the time of the lord Ahau Can of Chichén (1401), when Mayapán itself was destroyed by the rebellion of the people outside the city walls.

With respect to warfare —which was the means of obtaining greater economic surplusses from lands, products and force of labour— it is possible to distinguish a period dominated by the Itzá, from their arrival at Chichén until the date at which Mayapán declares war, 987 to 1185. This period of domination is reflected on the reliefs on the Ball Court, the Temple of the Bearded Man or the North Temple, the South Temple, the Substructure of the Warriors and the Substructure of the Castle. A second period is identifiable starting from the moment of the conquest of Chichén by Mayapán until the fall of the walled city, 1185 to 1401. This period is reflected in buildings such as the Castle, Temple of the Warriors and Annex of the Tigers, and on some painted murals and metal disks.

During the first period we see warriors with shirts or jackets with protective sleeves, as if puffed up, or filled out with cotton rings. They are wearing aprons or

88. Relief of a warrior in the Annex of the Tigers.

skirts, sandals with ankle straps, sometimes tied in the form of serpents, cotton capes decorated with beads and long feathered headdresses that fall down the backs or come out of the back of the helmets. They use horizontal, clay nose adornments, ear pieces, butterfly pectorals, helmets in the form of animals' heads, short feathered and raised headdresses sometimes with a butterfly pectoral or decoration on the front, back disks fixed to the belts and use eagle disguises or birds with curved beaks. There is a predominance of lance throwers or *átlatl*, these decorated with a large feather. They carry bunches of long darts or wooden staffs with one end curved and rectangular shields. All these elements are very similar to the attire of the ball game players who decorate the benches on the Ball Court.

During the second period the meshing or cotton mail-shirts *(ichcahuipillis)*, the headdresses in the style of diadems and mitres displaying a bird on the front are notable. The use of beards or moustaches, circular shields, lances, flags or insignias placed behind the backs *(pantemitl)*, standards depicting the figure of the deity of war, camps of huts or shelters with domed or conical roofs are all common features. These elements are characteristic of the Cocom of Mayapán, who with Mexican soldiers conquered Chichén Itzá *(Fig. 88)*.

On several of the gold disks extracted from the *cenote* or sacred well, the representation of a chief lord characterized by his beard and by the bird in front of his turban or headdress can be seen. This figure can be identified as Hunac Ceel, lord of the Cocom of Mayapán. On one of the disks this lord appears with a head band or turban with a bird on the front and plumes behind. He carries an *átlatl* which is adorned with a plume and two large darts. He has a beard, an ear piece and a bracelet with hanging ornaments. Sitting in front of him is a captive lord, with *ichcahuipilli* or cotton mail-shirt and a clay nose piece. Beside him is a receptacle containing the head of a decapitated victim. On each side of the lord is a warrior. One of these is brandishing a head cut by the hair. Above this scene is the serpent deity, and seated in one of the undulating curves of his body is the figure of a warrior, carrying an *átlatl* and a butterfly-shaped pectoral *(Fig. 89)*.

On another gold disk the same lord can be seen with the turban-bird and the cut or short feathers, with a circular shield and sling, and also with a type of moustache. At his feet sits another lord whose spear is pointing forwards. On either side of this lord is a warrior, in different attire and above these is the serpent deity, depicted realistically with forked tongue and rattlesnake rings on the tail *(Fig. 90)*.

From an interpretative point of view, it can be noted that on both disks the lord with the turban-bird (Kuk, Kukan, guacamaya bird) is represented and that he

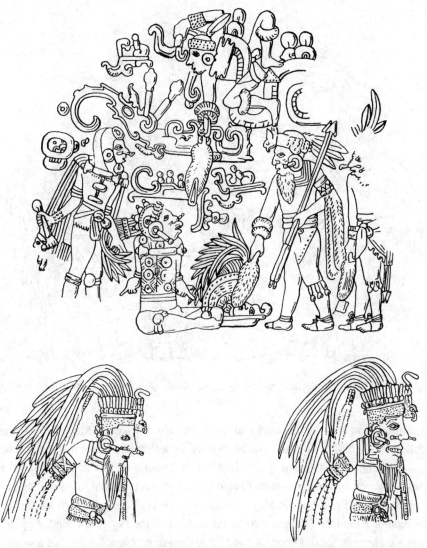

89. The Cocom, Hunac Ceel conquers Chichén Itzá. Disk in hammered gold
extracted from the Cenote.

is connected to the Cocom, and with Hunac Ceel of Mayapán. This lord has a
beard or moustache, which infers a connection with the cult to Ah Mex Cuc (of
the squirrel's beard). Hunac Ceel was his follower. It is also clear that a conquest
by war is implied as the vanquished lords are seated on the ground, there is decapitation and grasped hair and the spears are held out inclined to the front, symbolizing the surrender of arms, or the admission of their defeat.

90. The conquest of Chichén Itzá by Hunac Ceel. Gold disk extracted from the Cenote.

In this respect, it is necessary to recall that Hunac Ceel of Mayapán was the follower of Ah Mex Cuc, and that he "wished for a flower, a white mat, two dresses" (all the power, two lordships). Hunac Ceel conquered Chichén Itzá with the help of seven Mexican captains (Tzontecum, Pantemit, Itzcuat, etc.) and he became Ahau and priest of Ah Mex Cuc (of the squirrel's beard), perhaps a transformation of Kukulcán (Venus) into Itzam-ná (god of the sky or the sun). His cult has a preference for this concept and Hunac Ceel thus resembles the god and also the lord-high priest (Ah Mex Cuc) because of his beard.

Between 1185 and 1401 A. D. the scenes conmemorating the conquest of Chichén Itzá by the Cocom and their subsequent hegemony appear on the reliefs of some the buildings, in the metalurgy and on the painted murals, during the dictate of the conquerors from Mayapán. In the painting on the Temple of the Tigers one observes a hard fought battle on the outskirts of the city, with the village huts on fire, and the warriors with circular shields, slings, flags or insignia and standards *(Fig 91).*

91. Battle scene on a painted mural in the Temple of the Tigers.

This war extended to Izamal, which had links with Chichén Itzá. The *Chumayel* says: "the ruler of Izamal, Kinich Kakmoo as well as Pop-hol Chan was destroyed by Hunac Ceel...", and as a result the reign of the lord of Mayapán began: "Hunac Ceel, the sixth reign". The *Chumayel* continues, "obedience to the name of Ah Mex Cuc began...Then began the hearing of the prophecy, of the news, of the setting up of Ah Mex Cuc as he was called" and "then there was a change of katun, then there was a change of rulers/... Then began the idea of painting the exterior of the sun".

The religious aspect

Chichén Itzá had a tiered social structure with several different class levels, due to a complete division of labour, as the members of the work force carried out different specialized functions. This required a degree of social cohesion balancing the common interests with those of the elite and necessitating an independent solidarity, or, a degree of social conscience or sense of being part of, or belonging to, the society.

This also required the integration of the society with the State. It was necessary to develop an official ideology that would achieve the desired social cohesion and which could be transferred to the farthest and most outlaying parts of the region. This ideology was religion. It was elaborated by the priest who was dependent on the state apparatus, which together with the militarism assured the economical, political and psychological domination of the population.

Initially, the most important of the deities at Chichén Itzá was Kukulcán as he was the tribal god who created them and led them to the mouth of the well. It was he who measured and cleaned the lands where the Itzá settled, (the wise men of the water), and who at that time was called Mizcit Ahau. We have already remarked that this god was none other than Quetzalcóatl from the Central Mexican Altiplano, and he who had created the Fifth Sun and the new humanity, who discovered maize and agriculture, who was the inventor of the calendar and in general a benevolent god connected to Venus, who furthermore had four feet and two personalities (Nacxitl Quetzalcóatl).

The religion and cult to Kukulcán was a priestly elaboration originating in Xochicalco, Morelos. The cult was based on the mathematical calculations and astronomical observations achieved by the Maya, who fixed the cycle of Venus at

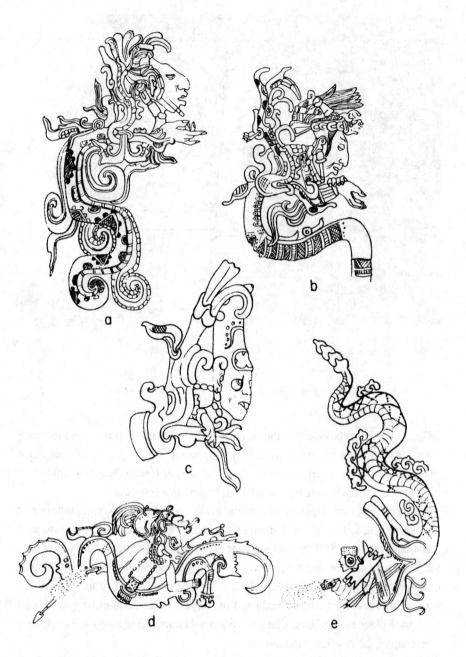

92. Representations of the god Kukulcán. a,b) Yaxchilán, Chiapas.
c) Copán, Honduras. d, e) Chichén Itzá.

93. Kukulcán. Panel on the Temple of the Warriors.

584 days. The symbol itself —the serpent-bird or plumed serpent— and its name comes from the green plumed quetzal (type of parrot) which was indigenous to the Maya world, and is referred to in the *Chilam Balam de Chumayel* as Yaxum (green bird, quetzal) and whose habitat was the mahogany tree *(caoba)*.

Quetzalcóatl was depicted in Xochicalco in a variety of ways, including as a lifelike serpent with feathers and cut conch shells, as a serpent out of whose jaws came the god, or as Tláloc, with the year glyph on his headdress, commonly seen in Yaxchilán, Uxmal and other Maya sites. In Chichén Itzá we find similar and other varieties, including lifelike serpents, the god coming out of the jaws of the serpent or intertwined with its body and the serpent in the form of hanging masks on square plaques or pillars. The decoration was enriched by the local craftsmen who adapted the new ideas to their art.

On some of the lintels in Yaxchilán, Chiapas, we find beautiful serpents from whose jaws the humanized god leaves. These lintels are all carved in the traditional artistic style of the Classic Maya. In Copán, Honduras, something similar occurs,

94. Temple of Venus: reliefs with the flower and the stone symbolizing Kukulcán.

but with the difference that here the god wears a four petalled flower on his fore-head. This symbol could refer either to Venus or to the Sun. On some of the gold disks extracted from the *cenote* or sacred well the deity is depicted as a warrior accompanied by a serpent, or coming out of the jaws of a rattlesnake *(Fig. 92)*.

Apart from these depictions, there are panels alluding to the god Kukulcán in Chichén. Kukulcán is often in the form of bird-serpents with long quetzal feathers and clawed feet, worked in bas-relief, and from whose sculptured and raised mouth rises the face of the god with a nose piece in the shape of a butterfly. Such panels in the Temple of the Warriors alternate with superimposed masks of Chac or god of the rain, the ancient deity of the site *(Fig 93)*.

95. Lintel showing the image of Kukulcán coming out of a serpent-bird. Temple of the Four Lintels.

This same realization is to be seen on the lower sections of the square pillars at Chichén Itzá, evoking the man-bird-serpent or Kukulcán. The association with Venus becomes clear on the decorations of the so called Temple of Venus, as there, the representation is of plumed serpents with rattlesnake tails and the god leaving the jaws of the serpent-bird, carrying the symbol of Pop. This symbol is a tied up stone, often a seat, which has a carving of the year hieroglyph (triangle-rectangle), together with a half flower of four petals, with four central petals and four outer petals (the four directions). Together, this symbolizes the power or dominion of Venus-Kukulcán *(Fig. 94)*.

An interesting realization is one which appears on the lintel of the Temple of the Four Lintels, situated in Old Chichén. Here, there is a quetzal bird with large plumes, with a disk on its body that has a four petalled flower. His head is a serpent from whose mouth emerges the god with a clay nose adornment. This representation is accompanied by fishes and birds, and also an illegible date. Its style still conserves some of the older artistic tradition from the time when the Itzá first introduced the cult to Kukulcán *(Fig 95)*.

With regard to this ancient representation and with the arrival of Kukulcán in the form of Lord of Time or of the Year, in turn related to rainfall, agriculture, the calendar, flora and fauna, we have already mentioned that in Uxmal he appears as a Tláloc with eye rings, moustache, fangs and the year hieroglyph in the headdress

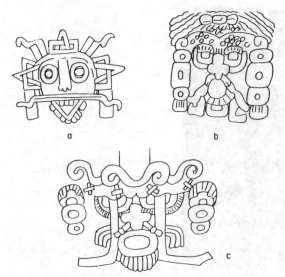

96. Masks alluding to Kukulcán: a) Uxmal. b) North Temple, Chichén Itzá. c) Annex of the Tigers, Chichén Itzá.

97. Drawing of a mask of Kukulcán, perhaps as Ah Mex Cuc (he of the squirrel's beard). Annex of the Tigers.

and the ear decoration. In Chichén Itzá however, this concept of the deity is enriched, as some of the characteristics (moustache, eye rings, fangs) are conserved, whilst others are added to form a beautiful and symbolical composition (Fig. 96).

On the pillars of the Annex to the Tigers we see this god with his nose in the form of a four petalled flower and with two splendid tubular beads (representing Venus), with eye rings, moustache, beard, decorated ear pieces, solar or star crosses

98. Detail of a mask of Kukulcán on the pillars of the Annex of the Tigers.

and tears falling from his eyes like waterfalls (water, rain). Around the sides of his face are plants with flowers, fishes, birds and turtles, the flora and fauna that is distributed in all the four directions of the earth. In this example the Venus deity or Kukulcán is related more closely to the Sun, the rain and the earth, and it is not unlikely that it is a representation of Ah Mex Cuc, (the one with the squirrel's beard) *(Figs. 97, 98).*

It can be deduced from the above examples that Kukulcán-bird-serpent represented the planet Venus and symbolized the light and the darkness, as both the morning star and the evening star. The deity is also related to the Sun, the wind, maize, vegetation, the rain and the animals. He is represented as an old man with a single tooth or with his teeth protruding, which has led to him being called 1 Ahau, patron of hunting. He was also known as Lahun Chan (Ten Sky, Ten Power) or god of the tenth sky, related to Venus. It is easy to confuse this deity with Itzam-ná as Kukulcán-Venus was also the creator of writing, of agriculture and other factors beneficial to man.

With regard to Itzam-ná (wise man of the sky and the clouds) he was represented as an old wizened man, with a roman nose and a single tooth, sometimes with a beard and with symbols in the form of a cross (sun) or flower (Venus), hence the confusion with Kukulcán. It is also said that he created writing in books or codexes, agriculture and medicine, these being attributes of a celestial and solar god. Itzam-ná was also called Itzamatul, Itzam Cab Aim (wise man who makes the rain;

wiseman-land-crocodile), as well as Itzamná Kauil or deity of the Four, of the cardinal points (or Amayté Kauil, of the four sides).

Another god was Kinich Kakmó (fire parrot with the solar face), also known as Kinchil Cobá (Grouse with solar face) and Kinich Ahau (Lord with face of the Sun), who represented the Sun. According to Cogulludo "at midday, in front of everyone, a fire descended that burned the sacrifice". Thus, the sun or fire bird descended so as to participate in the sacrificial acts being carried out in his name. The same deity, indeed, who according to the *Chumayel* had his altar and was adored in Izamal and Cozumel.

Of course, in Chichén Itzá the cult to Chac or god of the rain and associated phenomena continued, as can be seen in the masks decorating the temple of the Warriors, The Caracol and the Castle. These show the reptilian attributes and rolled up nose like a trunk associated with Chac. He was protector of agriculture. Chac had four helpers or Chaques related to the cardinal points and their colours, who were worshiped by the people as they represented the slashing and burning of the milpa, the sowing, the fruiting and the harvest.

It is thought that four brothers who had levelled the world when the earth and the firmament sank, the Bacabes, supported the sky by its four corners. Their names were Chac Xib Chac (in the east and coloured red), Zac Xib Chac (in the north and white) Ek Xib Chac (in the west and black) and Kan Xib Chac (in the south and yellow). We have also already mentioned the Pauah or Pauahtunes who were the kings or custodians of the rains of the four directions. These were Red Pauah (east), White Pauah (north), Black Pauah (west) and Yellow Pauah (south).

This four part pattern that ruled for the Chaques, Bacabes, Iques and Pahuatunes, extended to the four ceiba trees or the original trees of the world. Chac Imix Ché, Zak Imix Ché, Ek Imix Ché and Kan Imix Ché. In this example there was also the Great Mother Ceiba of the centre, or Yaax Imix Ché (green). This tree was associated with the birds, maintenance, stones, bees (men) and with the bearers of time or the year and the Ah Toc or four calendar gods (4 Chicchán, 4 Oc, 4 Men y 4 Ahau).

In the *Chumayel* the Oxlahun-ti-kú or thirteen gods of the light or of the thirteen upper skies are named and these ruled the basic thirteen. The Bolon-ti-kú or nine gods of the night or of the darkness; the god Ah Puch or Yum Kimil, lord of the underworld (of the dead); Ix Tab goddess of the rope, patron of the hanged; and the god Ek Chuuah (black scorpion or non venenous scorpion) who was the patron of the merchants and related to the Pole Star (Xaman Ek) or guiding star for the merchants. He was also linked with the gods of war (Kakupakat, Ah Chuy Kak and others).

As we have said previously, the priest possessed astronomical, mathematical, calendaric and astrological knowledge. He was responsible for religion, cults and rites and ceremonies. He fasted, made auto-sacrifices, offered prayers and made offerings in the temples. At the festivities held in the squares there was never a shortage of music, dance and other amusements, such as the Ball Court. There were also human sacrifices (like those of the *cenote* or sacred well), in which the chosen victim (children or adults, men or women) was carried in procession, purified in the *temazcal* or steam bath that was on the mouth of the well, then after being bathed, was richly attired and sacrificed on the platform beside the *temazcal*, finally being flung into the water of the well beneath, accompanied by the offerings for the god who dwelled within.

Clothing and Ornaments

In the bas-reliefs, paintings and other works of art, apart from the warriors already described, we see ball game players who wear shirts with protective sleeves, skirts or aprons, breeches with the ends decorated, collars-capes decorated with beads or *chalchihuites* and sandals with ankle straps. They use simple knee bands sometimes with a disk on the front, wide belts like yokes with "palmas" in front and back disks with hanging plumes. There are peaks of feathers behind the back or coming out of their helmets or turbans. Their long hair is tied in a pony tail and both head and hair is covered with helmets in animal forms, turbans adorned with disks and flowers and different kinds of zoomorfic emblems or insignia, formed in the shape of a padlock. There are the standard clay nose pieces, ear plugs, pectorals in the shape of a cut shell, necklaces of beads, bracelets and straps or bandages on the knees.

In the North Temple the principal lord is depicted wearing a tunic covered with beads or *chalchihuites*. There are other individuals wearing capes, butterfly pectorals, rigid or cut feather headdresses and bird disguises. There are also realizations of women with long hair, wearing petticoats or skirts and huipiles. They are adorned with bracelets, their hair is gathered up and they wear circular ear and other adornments.

In the Temple of the Warriors is a painting of the lord Chac Xib Chac, dressed

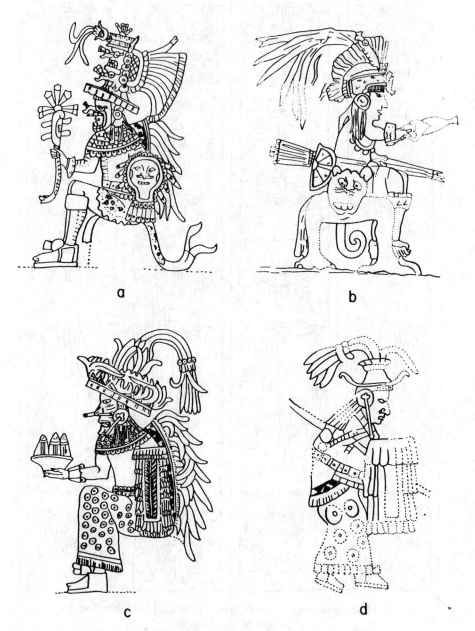

99. Clothing of important people in Chichén Itzá: a) Chac Xib Chac. b) Warrior.
c) Priest. d) Wise man. Temple of the Warriors.

100. Clothing of some of the figures at Chichén Itzá. Pillar from the temple of the Warriors.

in a jaguar skin skirt, woven shirt, belt, collar-cape with precious stones and sandals with ankle straps. He has a feathered headdress on his helmet with the heads of the solar god or god of the rain. It is adorned with feathers and a lotus flower on the front. The warrior also uses clay nose pieces, circular ear adornments, wrist decorations, a hand staff with flint or obsidian edges, finished off as a serpent, and a shield decorated with feathers and beads *(Fig. 99a)*.

From the paintings on the same building is the representation of a warrior seated on a jaguar throne. There is also a depiction of a priest wearing a skirt decorated with *chalchihuites* or precious stones, collar-cape, clay nose adornment and a beautiful feathered headdress. There is a visualization possibly of a wise man or conjuror, wearing a skirt and cape *(Fig. 99 b, c, d)*.

On the many square pillars of the Temple of the Warriors are realizations of priests, warriors and important figures, who wear butterfly pectorals, or pectorals in the form of a human face surrounded by precious stones and beautiful feathers (like suns). They also have clay nose adornments and ear plugs, necklaces of precious stones sometimes with a serpent hanging at the neck, turbans with birds or serpents on the front and helmets in the form of fantastic birds. They are wearing skirts, belts and have back disks. Some individuals, wearing long skirts adorned with precious stones, hats and with receptacles in their hands, may well be merchants. Of course, on the lower part of each pillar Kukulcán appears leaving the jaws of a serpent-bird, with a forked tongue coming out of his mouth and with a butterfly nose adornment. On the upper sections are the warriors marked with solar rays, in groups of four, possibly indicating the directions of the world *(Figs. 100, 101)*.

There is no doubt that the class that held power and ruled the society was the best dressed and the most elaborately adorned. They used the finest raw materials and luxurious or sumptuous manufactured goods, obtained by tributes and by conquering villages and towns, and also through commercial interchanges from the artisan surplus of the city. A large part of the clothing, adornments and jewels of the upper class were imported, either in the form of fine and exotic materials or as manufactured goods.

In Chichén Itzá wide and long loincloths or breeches (ex) were commonly used. These were in the form of a band wrapped several times around the waist and then passed between the legs, with one end hanging down at the front and one behind, like an apron. Sometimes the breeches were decorated with coloured threads or plumes. Also common were short skirts coming to half way down the thigh held with a belt woven in cotton, or made of jaguar skin. Capes were adorned with feathers and long shirts, like tunics reaching knee length or below, were trimmed with precious stones or *chalchihuites*, or tooled with beautiful drawings. They wore a type of knee length jacket and ankle length skirts and sometimes a *huipil* over a shift or petticoat. Other clothing included fringed cloths and sandals with ankle straps, made of leather or *henequén*.

They also wore hats, turbans, diadems or tiaras, feathered headdresses (guacamaya, quetzal, parrot, lark, cardenal), paper adornments, flowers and birds. Disks made of mosaic of turquoise, shell, obsidian and pyrites were used in decoration. Nose adornments, pectorals, bracelets, ear decorations and necklaces were made of a variety of precious metals and stones including jade, gold, copper, silver, amber, rock crystal and wood. Other acessories included fans, sceptres or staffs and offensive and defensive weapons.

There is no doubt that personal attire and adornment required many of the prime materials available. Of these the most important were cotton, *henequén*, "palmas", skins, feathers, dyes, jade, bone, wood, shells and sea snails, pyrites, turquoise, amber, metals, rock crystal, obsidian and flint. To exploit these materials there were specialist craftsmen such as weavers, skin curers, engravers, plumists, gold and silversmiths, painters, stonemasons and many others, as well as the professional merchants.

Commerce

Chichén Itzá was the leading city of the region in religion, cults, festivals and commercial activities. Chichén controlled and redistributed goods and services between the neighbouring regions such as Mayapán and Izamal, by maintaining control over the prime materials and regional domestic products, and also the local craft production. Within the city were professional or full time merchants who exported part of their produce and imported what was lacking, always taking account of supply and demand of particular goods that were commonly interchanged between different towns and villages, and of the people with buying power.

The merchants who travelled far afield belonged to the upper classes. Often the lords themselves and some of their family would be involved in this activity, although there would also be smaller merchants or intermediaries who redistributed the produce and prime materials in the local markets and in the nearby communi-

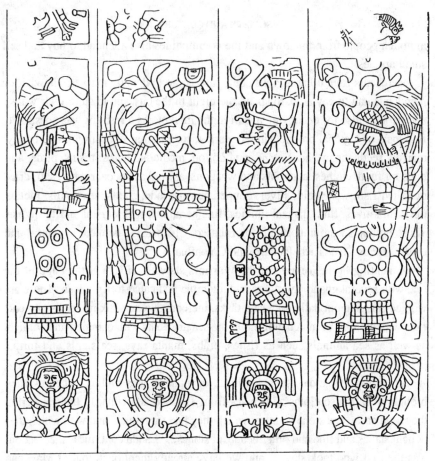

101. Pillar from the temple of the Warriors.

ties. Some regulations and agreements governing the conduct of interchanges and monetary units or value already existed, amongst these the precious stones or coloured shells (Kan), certain cotton cloths of a fixed size, copper bells (cascabel) and pincers or hand axes, jade stones, quetzal feathers and cocoa beans, which were the most coveted.

In general, the merchants carried a fan, walking stick and a bag as trademark to their profession. They were accompanied by carriers who carried the merchandise and they sometimes had a military escort. They used natural paths and artificial roads or *sacbés*, constructed by the governors of the principal cities. The merchandise was exchanged or sold in the city market which was held on special days and on the important religious festivals, under the supervision of the market's judges, although people from the town and the communities also attended to buy and sell small articles.

Merchants from other regions could also come to the city market. The visiting merchants had to pay a tax to spend the night in the city and to store their wares, and perhaps also for occupying a stall in the market. As a result it was possible to find local or regional products in the market, such as maize, beans, chillie, honey, marrow seeds, hemp, *henequén,* spun cotton, medicinal herbs, resins, birds, animals for food, clothes, materials and weapons, as well as cocoa, rubber, salt, dried or salted fish, wax, gold, silver, copper, jewels, jade, shells, sea snails, metals, obsidian knives, flint, quetzal plumes, fine ceramics, rock crystal and turquoise. These products were imported from Tabasco, Chiapas, Guatemala, Honduras and even as far as Costa Rica, Panamá and Colombia.

A painting in the Temple of the Warriors shows a village at the edge of the sea, with several guano palm huts and a temple dedicated to Kukulcán. There are women carrying out daily domestic tasks, merchants with walking sticks and carriers with bundles of merchandise. On the sea are boats with oarsmen and soldiers as well as sea animals such as fishes, crabs, manta rays, sea snails and turtles *(Fig. 102).*

According to Landa, "their favourite occupation was trading, whereby they brought in salt; also cloths and slaves from Tabasco and Ulúa. In their bartering they used cacao and stone counters which they had for money, and with which they bought slaves and fine and other beautiful stones..." Landa continues "that Cocom was the first who took slaves" and we have already mentioned that in Mayapán there were houses outside the city wall where the lords of other regions kept servants, and where the people from their towns and villages resided on arrival in the city on commercial and other business.

Handcrafts

The material evidence that has come from Chichén Itzá reveals the existence of several skills or crafts carried out by full time residents of the city, perhaps occupying particular districts or regions of the city. It is likely that they possessed their own tools but prime materials and production were controlled by the State. Amongst these craftsmen we can mention the incense (copal) and rubber producers, whose prime material was obtained from commercial interchanges, but then trans-

102. Painting from the Temple of the Warriors showing a commercial scene.

formed into products fundamentally for use at religious cults or festivals.

The copal (pom) whilst in its plastic state was put in vases or baskets to set so that when firm it took the form of the receptacle. Sometimes it was set on leaves whose veins would then remain impressed on the copal. It could also be moulded into balls or into stylized human figures. Generally, inside the mass of copal were green stones and tiny tips of projectiles, which can only be seen by radiography or by breaking open the resin. The craftsmen also used to superficially interleave small figurines and small rubber balls, with the intention of burning these first when they were thrown to the sacred well as an offering *(Figs. 103, 104)*.

The rubber (kik) was used as fuel for the copal and could be modelled in the form of human figures or little balls which were attached to the mass of resin or "supreme, heavenly perfume". This was the material used for the solid balls that were used in the Ball Court, made either on site or imported in commerce.

The craftsmen also made some small wooden sculptures that they covered with a layer of rubber and copal. These had very stylized human characteristics and also

103. Vessel with rubber and incense (copal), taken from the Cenote.

104. Mass of incense (copal) in the form of a receptacle, with the impression of a leaf.

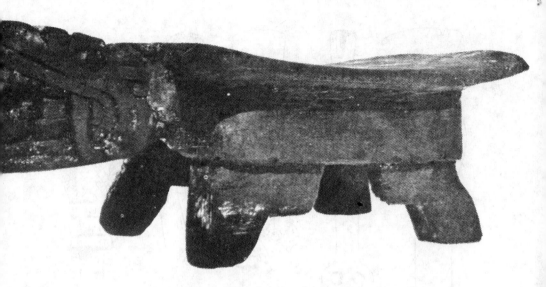

105. Small bench with the effigy of Kukulcán coming out of the jaws of a serpent.
This was salvaged from the Cenote.

served as offerings to be thrown into the sacrifical well. With regard to the wood, the gum tree (chicozapote) lintels forming entrances on the buildings can also be mentioned. The canoas and oars seen on the murals, the framework of some shields, the bases of the pyrites mosaic mirrors and the staffs and sceptres perhaps with curved ends, decorated with gods and finished with a serpent, were also made of wood.

The slings or arrow throwers (hulche) were also made of wood. These had two wings with holes for the fingers and a curved butt inside to detain the wooden arrow and were sometimes decorated with figures or with a feather. Machete type weapons were made out of the edge of flint or obsidian, incrusted and anointed with resins. The handles of the sacrificial knives, in the form of intertwining serpents, and also the handles of the fans were made of wood. Other articles include spears and javelins with flintstone ends, and small four legged benches with the effigy of Kukulcán on one end, that were used for the sacrificial ceremony at the holy well. There were also spatulas, bobbins for weaving and spinning, ear adornments, rings, perhaps rings worn on the lower lip, rattles and even bells (cascabeles) *(Figs. 105, 106)*.

Fragments of simple weave textiles with complicated pictures have been re-

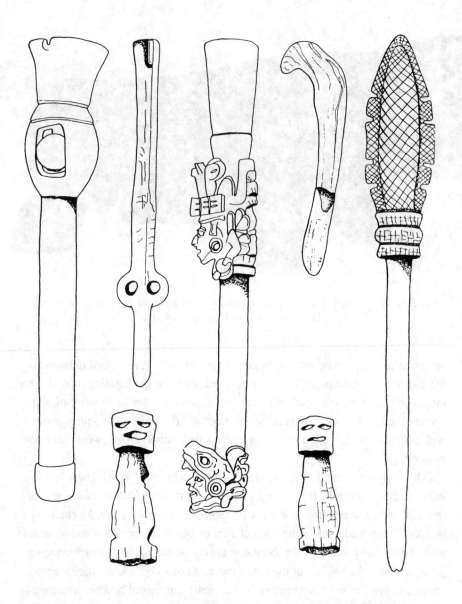

106. Wooden objects taken from the Cenote: rattle, hulché or dart-thower, hand staffs or sceptres, stick for throwing, human figures.

107. Sandal taken from the Cenote.

moved from the sacred well, indicating several elaborate techniques which can also be observed in the clothing as seen on the bas-reliefs already described. Fragments of ropes and cords, *petates* (straw mats) and baskets have been found indicating the development of the weaving and basket making. These were made from such materials as cotton, henequén or sisal and bark, and woven using waist looms *(Fig. 107).*

Several pieces of earthenware have also been extracted from the well, not only revealing different types of pottery or ceramics but also indicating the chronological development of Chichén Itzá, from 650 A. D. when offerings were made to the god of rain until the change in practice to make human sacrifices to the cult of Kukulcán in 1350 A. D. Of the pottery found we can mention grey coloured vessels with black, dripping paint (Pizarra Media), principally pots with side handles, simple pots and pots with a ridge or superficial rim, casseroles with strengthened edges, fine grey ceramics, pots of a fine cream colour, sometimes with decoration on both facets and many others indicating the later part of the boom or classic period (650-1000 A. D.).

There are also small three legged plates and simple bowls painted blue and often with copal decoration. There are white or ivory ceramics with black, dripping paint (Pizarra Tardía), greyish pots with black paint and ear-like handles on the edge, red, highly polished pots, fine orange ceramics, pots with deep rims or ridges, tripod pots with supports and coffee coloured or reddish incisions and a rattle, lead coloured ceramics, fragments of urns with a profusion of very fine ornaments, and of stoves and incense burners pertaining to the Mayapán period. Corresponding to the Mesoamerican Post Classic period when the Itzá occupied the site (1000 - 1400 A. D.) are pots with effigies, rough reddish ceramics, sharp machete type weapons and late orange ceramics.

Typical of the fine and semi-precious stone work are plaques with bas-reliefs work, carved and engraved pectorals, ear adornments, small figures and heads to use as pendants, necklaces of precious stones and other small objects tooled in jade and other greenish stones. There were pots worked in transparent marble or alabaster and some of these show the remains of painting. Other articles include triangular projectile tips with ridges and rectangular stems, made of chalcedony, flint and obsidian, and flint knives and obsidian daggers. Mosaic work was commom with articles such as pyrites mirrors on mosaic bases and small sections of turquoise mosaic and also irregular or eccentric-shaped obsidian objects. They even used perforated conch shells to hang from the pectorals and geometric plaques or plaques in the form of figures to be sewn on to the clothing as well as beads and cut shells (the symbol of the wind), and other decorative objects made from shells and sea snails such as Spondylus Crassisquana, Fasciolaria, Strombus, Busycon, Pinctada and Oliva *(Fig. 108)*.

Deer bone was also tooled to make needles and daggers, sometimes taken from the antlers themselves. Large human bones were cut and incised with decorations. Some human skulls were also prepared with incrustations in place of the eyes. Many of the brightly coloured feathers were used, as also sharks teeth, rabbit skins, animal fangs, rock crystal, amber, turtle carapaces and *cocoyol* seed. Bark of the *amate* tree was used for making paper.

During the Itzá supremacy, the knowledge of metalurgy was introduced into Chichén Itzá, due to the connections between the Yucatan Penínsular, Honduras, Costa Rica, Panamá and Colombia and particularly via the Caribbean. In this way, prime material could be received and then transformed into manufactured articles by the metal workers in the city. All was achieved by means of commerce.

Gold objects (takin) have been extracted from the cenote or sacred well, as well as copper (mazcab), copper mixed with tin (zac tau), copper with lead (ek tau) and silver (zac takin). Other objects made of gold, silver and copper alloys were also removed. The fine hammering of these metals must also be admired, as well as the moulding and melting of the wax moulds, the beating, soldering, gold-plating and false filigrée work. The objects display a variety of styles from the Central High-

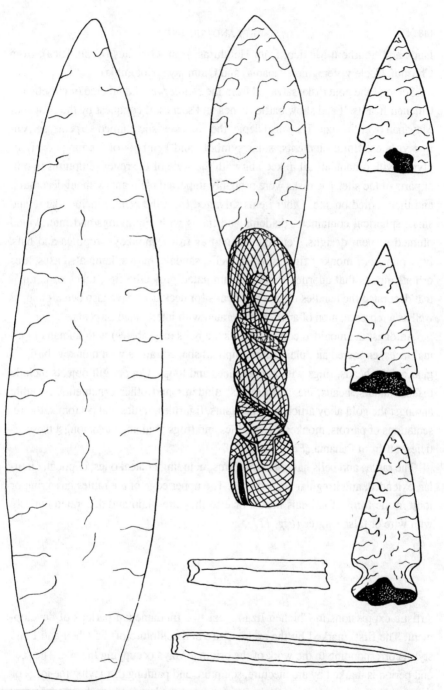

108. Objects tooled in Obsidian: sacrifical knives, projectile tips and daggers.
From the Sacred Well.

lands and Southern Mexico, from Honduras, from Guapiles (Costa Rica), from Chiriquí, Coclé y Veraguas (Panamá) and Quimbaya (Colombia).

Some of the gold disks salvaged from the *cenote* were hammered or chiselled in Chichén Itzá itself and show battle scenes and scenes of conquest by the people of Mayapán over the Itzá. They also depict the characteristic plumed serpents, serpentine volutes, floral elements, solar symbols and symbols of Venus and hieroglyphs with ornaments all in keeping with the style of the relief sculptures in other parts of the site. The disks were probably imported plain and without decoration and then tooled on site. Other items salvaged from the *cenote* include large and small spherical containers, diadems and tiaras with engravings and intertwined plumed serpent designs. Pendants shaped as frogs, monkeys, reptiles and bats, little human or monkey figures, rings, bells, sandals, masks, laminated asps, arcs or half moons that adorned the nose, laminated projectile tips, tubes or laminas that decorated the handles of fans and beads for necklaces have also been found, as well as a representation of an *átlatl* decorated with intertwined serpents.

Amongst the moulded copper objects are bells (cascabeles) with human or animal faces, engraved and plain rings, eliptical shaped rattles with monkey, bird, jaguar or dog heads, rings with human faces and loops. Copper gilt objects include disks, sandals, beads, ear adornments, diadems and other ornaments. Notable amongst the gold alloy articles are pendants, figurines, rattles and pectorals. Representations of parrots, monkeys, crocodiles and frogs predominate amongst these articles, all from Panamá *(Figs. 109, 110)*.

The rattles and bells have several forms including conical ones, eliptical, circular, extended, and irregular shaped ones. The upper edge of the rattles has a ring or loop in the form of animals heads, or else they are plain and decorated entirely with wire or false filigrée *(Fig. 111)*.

Art

Artistic expressions in Chichén Itzá reveal two fundamental periods of development. The first, marked by the architecture and sculpture of the Chen and Puuc styles corresponding to the work of the original Maya occupying the site. The second period is marked by architecture, sculpture and painting displaying the ideas of the Itzá, in the Maya-Yucatec style. This style, in the hands of local and traditional artists, incorporates some of the ancient elements.

109. Copper-gilt sandals found in the Cenote.

Architecturally the city began to spread southwards, towards the *cenote* Xtoloc which provided the drinking water. The buildings were still built largely in a disperse way but included some small groups of ceremonial and civil buildings, such as the Nunnery, the Church and East Annex. This provided a fairly homogeneous base but with some relatively isolated buildings such as the Chichanchob or Red House, the House of the Deer, the Akabdzib, the Three Lintels and others.

These buildings show a combination of architectural and sculptural design. The decoration of the facades was sometimes complete like the Chen style, or parcial, covering the frieze alone as in the Puuc style. The decoration was made of finely cut stone mosaic, tooled, assembled and adjusted carefully, as well as using stucco and some painting. The decoration was geometrical and combined rectangular fret patterns, panels of cross-hatching, masks of Chac, little drums and columns, split columns on the corners and dados of inverted and chevron patterned triangles.

It was customary to construct buildings on low platforms and plinths and to use masonry and vaulted roofs or the Maya false arch. Apparently, the ceremonial

and religious buildings dominated the other stuctures on the site. There was a clear
distinction between the governors' houses and those of the rest of the population
and the local and neighbouring labour force was employed for the extension of the
centre. This construction work was organized and in the hands of town planners
who designed the buildings and others who extracted and transported the material
(stone, lime, white, clayish soil (cascab), water, dung, wood). Other labourers
mixed the lime, cleared and levelled the plots, set the stones or walls, tooled and
worked the blocks and smoothed the floors and walls. These were, in fact, the ar-
chitects, site formen, labourers, quarrymen, masons, carpenters and sculptors.

Although the Itzá introduced new architectural, religious and artistic ideas, it
was important for them to engage the local craftsmen and artists, on whom they
depended to carry out their ideas. At this time the northern part of the city was also
developed near the sacred or sacrificial well. The Itzá influence spread back into the
old city so as to have better control over the population, incorporating the work-
force into certain public works projects. The Itzá were also supported by the armed
forces.

The concept of the sloping elevation and the vertical wall was introduced in the
architecture, as also the use of columns with capitals, bases and platforms with
four stairs, circular buildings and crenels finishing off the roofs of the buildings.
These elements in turn gave way to the serpentine columns, porticos and benches.
Both sculpture and the painted murals were dedicated to the religion to Kukulcán
and to militarism.

In accordance with the interests of the ruling class, and to secure a degree of social cohesion, they planned and built the internal road networks linking the suburbs or groups to the principal ceremonial centre. This increased the affluance of
the people (easier communications) and facilitated pilgramages, festivities and access for the collection of tributes in food or raw materials. Large bases were built
for the buildings and modifications were made to some ancient structures, adding
particular religious elements or sculptures to the facades. Painted murals were added to the buildings and sculpture imitations of which can be seen in the metalurgy.

Thus, Chichén Itzá, the city of the wise men of the water, clearly illustrates
the cultural progress achieved in architecture, public works, religion, sculpture, ceramics and metalurgy. One must also marvel at the achievements of the Itzá in the
fields of astronomy, mathematics, calendars, history, geography, botany and medicine, all knowledge acquired by the Balams or priests of those times. By means of
the Chilam Balam and the codexes the Itzá contributed directly to the perpetuation

110. Zinc and copper alloy
figurine, from Panamá.
This was salvaged from
the Cenote.

of their songs and narrative tradition. In the *Chumayel* we read: "<This is> the history of the world in those times, because it has been written down, because the time has not yet ended for making these books, these many explanations..."

This short essay is as if a small part of "the record of the things which they did. After it had all passed, they told it in their <own> words .... everything shall be thoroughly explained [again]..." perhaps even more clearly, to better understand "how to explain these things when he reads [it is read] what is here".

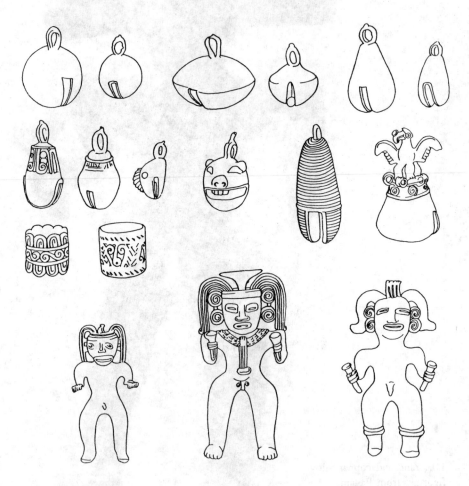

111. Different types of bell (casacabel), rings and figurines, brought to Chichén Itzá through commerce. From the Cenote.

BIBLIOGRAPHY AND INDEX

BIBLIOGRAFIA

Barrera Vázquez, Alfredo y Silvia Rendón
    1948.— *El libro de los Libros de Chilam Balam*. Biblioteca Americana. Fondo de Cultura Económica.

Códice Chimalpopoca
    1945.— *Anales de Cuauhtitlán y Leyenda de los Soles*. U.N.A.M., México.

Historia Tolteca-Chichimeca
    1947.— *Anales de Quauhtinchan*. México.

Landa, Fray Diego de.
    1938.— *Relación de las Cosas de Yucatán*. Versión de Héctor Pérez Martínez. México.

Lothrop, S. kirkland.
    1952.— "Metals from the Cenote of Sacrifice, Chichen Itza, Yucatan." *Peabody Museum*. Vol. X. Núm. 2. Cambridge.

Marquina, Ignacio.
    1951.— "Arquitectura Prehispánica." *Memorias, 1*. I.N.A.H., México.

Mediz Bolio, Antonio.
    1973.— *Libro de Chilam Balam de Chumayel*. Biblioteca del Estudiante Universitario. U.N.A.M., México.

Parsons, Lee A.
    1969.— "Bilbao, Guatemala: An Archaeological Study of the Pacific Coast, Cotzumalhuapa Region." *Milwaukee Public Museum*. Pub. in Anthropology. Núm. 12, Vol. 2. Wisconsin.

Piña Chan Román

1963.— "Informe Preliminar sobre Mul Chic, Yucatán." Anales del I.N.A.H.
    Tomo XV. México.

1964.— "Algunas Consideraciones sobre Mul Chic, Yucatán." Estudios de
    Cultura Maya. Vol. IV. U.N.A.M. México.

1970.— "Informe de la Reciente Exploración del Cenote Sagrado de Chichén
    Itzá", Serie Investigaciones. Núm. 24. I.N.A.H. México.

1972.— *Historia, Arqueología y Arte Prehispánico.* Fondo de Cultura Econó-
    mica. México.

Recinos, Adrián.

1947.— *Popol Vuh: Las Antiguas Historias del Quiché.* Biblioteca Americana.
    Fondo de Cultura Económica. México.

1950.— *Memorial de Sololá.* Biblioteca Americana. Fondo de Cultura Econó-
    mica. México.

Roys, R. L.

1933.— *The Book of Chilam Balam of Chumayel.* Carnegie Inst. of Washing-
    ton. Pub 438. Washington.

Stephens, J. L.

1843.— *Incidents of Travel in Yucatan.* 2 Vols. New York and London.

Thompson, J. Eric S.

1970.— *Maya History and Religion.* Norman, Oklahoma.

Tozzer, Alfred M.

1957.— "Chichen Itza and its Cenote of Sacrifice: a comparative study of con-
    temporaneus Maya and Toltec." *Peabody Museum.* Cambridge.

Willard, Teodore A.

1926.— *The City of the Sacred Well.* The Century Co. New York.

INDEX

SOCIETY AND CULTURE

Esta edición consta de 1,000 ejemplares
impresos en diciembre de 1996, en los
talleres de **Litoarte, S.A. de C.V.**
San Andrés Atoto No. 21-A,
Col. Industrial Atoto, Nauc.
53519, Estado de México

Esta edición consta de 1000 ejemplares
impresos en diciembre de 1998 en los
talleres de Impresora A. de C.V.,
San Andrés Atoto, C.A.,
Col. Industrial Atoto, Naucalpan,
53519 Estado de México.